A VERY
GAY BOOK

A VERY GAY BOOK

AN INACCURATE RESOURCE FOR GAY SCHOLARS

NIC SCHEPPARD and JENSON TITUS

Andrews McMeel
PUBLISHING®

A VERY GAY BOOK

Andrews McMeel Publishing
a division of Andrews McMeel Universal
1130 Walnut Street, Kansas City, Missouri 64106

www.andrewsmcmeel.com

23 24 25 26 27 IGO 10 9 8 7 6 5 4 3 2 1

ISBN: 978-1-5248-7644-9

Library of Congress Control Number: 2022949670

Editors: Allison Adler, Betty Wong
Art Director: Holly Swayne
Production Editor: Meg Utz
Production Manager: Chadd Keim

Illustrations on pages x, 3, 4, 6, 10, 12, 15, 17, 20, 72, 82-83,
103, 109, 133 copyright © 2023 by Bradley Clayton.

ATTENTION: SCHOOLS AND BUSINESSES
Andrews McMeel books are available at quantity discounts with bulk purchase for
educational, business, or sales promotional use. For information, please e-mail
the Andrews McMeel Publishing Special Sales Department: sales@amuniversal.com.

This book is dedicated to:
Melissa's Sister.

Thank you for all you've done/sacrificed, etc.

CONTENTS

SCIENCE

IS GAY . . . 93

HOW TO USE THIS BOOK

You're going to want to read this book in a way that is gay.

Please don't read this in any sort of straight way.

Don't read this book at an Irish-themed sports bar or a gender-reveal party. Don't read it while enjoying an album by the Foo Fighters or putting your three-year-old son in a "Ladies' Man" onesie. And, God, we are BEGGING you not to read this through a pair of Oakley sunglasses unless you are doing it with a wink—in sort of a hot, queer, ironic way.

This book is divided into sections, and we'd like to say that each is gayer than the last, but we ended up making them all so gay. We won't prescribe an ideal sequence for you to read it in, because we know your gay ass is going to do whatever the hell you want. We're done trying to argue with you. God, you are exhausting.

This is a reference book, so bear in mind that everything included herein has been thoroughly researched and peer-reviewed. Also, bear in mind that the two of us are at the top of our game, so our only peers are one another. We've reviewed each other's contributions to the text and find it all to be awesome and true. That should be enough.

You may be thinking as you read that broad, overarching statements about queerness and sexuality are reductive and harmful. That they don't allow for nuance or individuality. If this is a concern of yours, you must be gay. All gay people are discerning.

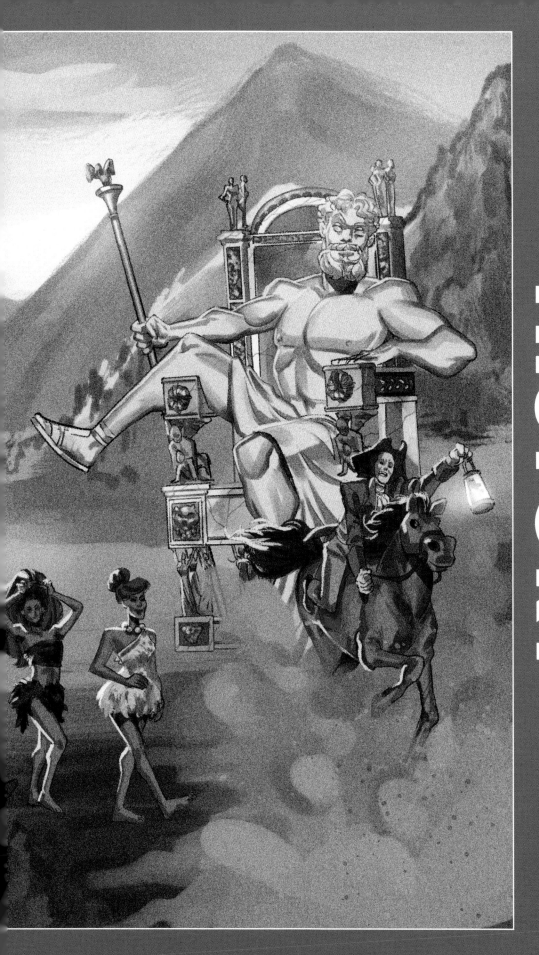

HISTORY

IS GAY

GENESIS

In the beginning, there was nothing. Then, it was gay.

We'll need to change a few names here to protect identities, but the first few days of creation went as follows:

1. PAUL created light. PAUL saw the light bouncing around and thought how cool it would be later when he created mirrors, sequins, and photography courses. He liked it. And it was gay.

2. PAUL created the sky and thought, "There are going to be so many songs about putting your hands up here." PAUL saw that those songs, the hands, and the sky were all gay.

3. On the third day, PAUL started to get really into having a lot of plants. He kept calling himself a "plant dad," even though there was no one around yet to listen to him. He laughed to himself at how funny he thought the term "plant dad" was. And that was gay.

4. PAUL made the rest of the solar system on the fourth day. He was particularly concerned with the sun, which he made very big and *very* gay, but he also hid that part from the sun so it could go on its own journey to realize its gayness and learn a lot of other lessons about love and life along the way. He liked that sort of story structure, and he saw that it was gay.

5. The following day, PAUL made sea creatures and birds, mostly because these would inspire a lot of great costumes to be worn by what he would create the following day, which were . . .

6. People. People were created with an incredible aptitude for being gay and doing gay things. PAUL started to plan on this day for all the very gay people he would make in the future. He got the idea for Wanda Sykes on this day, and though he waited a while to put the plan into action, Wanda was one of his favorite ideas and he spent a lot of this day getting excited about how cool she would be. He also created land mammals, who would inspire some less-exciting costumes from the people, but costumes nonetheless. And it was gay.

PAUL'S FAVORITE

7. On the seventh day, PAUL just sort of had brunch, and that was kind of it.

PREHISTORIC GAYS

Paleontology, the study of prehistoric life, is the gayest science of them all. Paleontologists make sweeping assumptions based on little to no evidence: the foundation of all gay thought. From the creation of fire, which allowed queers to show off rare bone jewelry at night, to the invention of the screwdriver (vodka orange), gays have been around since Donna Time, the very first drag queen. Despite today's cultural understanding, "Prehistorics" are not gay men in their 30s but are actually some of the first gay humans to have existed on the Earth.

Here are some of the most important inventions from Prehistoric Gays:

Slinging Something over Your Shoulder: Invented by a gay man who needed both hands to tell his little story.

Hiding from Reptiles: Being afraid of reptiles has not only saved countless lives but is also gay.

Flossing: A prehistoric lesbian invented flossing.

Singing: This was actually invented by a prehistoric gay bird and was later adapted by a man for whom words were not enough to express the emotions he was feeling.

Musical Theater: Created by the above man who was, by far, the most annoying person to be around in prehistory.

Jogging a Little Bit after You Trip: This bisexual woman later went on to invent running simply because she could never admit she tripped over that rock.

THE SEVEN WONDERS OF THE ANCIENT GAY WORLD

These gay landmarks have stood the test of time, and for good reason! While many are household names, it's important that we include them here to give a comprehensive look at where we've come from and where we're going.

1. Spiral Staircases (all of them): There is an ancient gay energy contained in every spiral staircase. The subversion of expectation in making a staircase circle back on itself is one of the purest examples of gay influence in architecture.
2. The Redwood Forests of Northern California: It's no coincidence that these iconic titans of Nature are mentioned in one of America's gayest songs, "This Land is Your Land." Redwoods are as old as they are gay.
3. The Set of *Full House*: Three single men living together in San Francisco? Now, c'mon now.
4. The River Thames: The way you are supposed to pronounce this river's name was changed after the MAYOR (yes) of London had a nasty breakup with a man named James and didn't want to be reminded of him every time the river was referenced. We recognize this adjustment as fair and understandable.
5. Season One of *Big Little Lies*: It's been eons since this gift to the gay community was seemingly dropped into our laps by the gods. Like the pyramids, no one is quite sure how this was organized in a time when resources and technology were so different from today. Maybe help from aliens. Maybe a bending of time and space. Either way, it is a gift that a long-forgotten culture left for us, and our job may not be to understand, it may just be to give thanks.
6. The Mighty Gagotrondra: The first Viking ship. It is said that the serpent's head on the bow originally wore a chunky statement necklace that has been lost to time. Treasure hunters are as eager to find what has been described as "a necklace similar to what Mrs. Darbus from *High School Musical* would wear but very, very big" as they are to find the Ark of the Covenant.
7. Santa's Village: Known as the West Hollywood of the North, this icy paradise welcomes tens of thousands of gay vacationers each month. The northern lights and their strange effect on technology have prevented any photo documentation of this location, but there exist many *Titanic*–style hand-drawn pictures of nude men lying on piles of presents.

OREGON TRAIL

The drama. The longing. The desire.

It all began in 1811, with a prominent group of socialites called the "Trailblazers." The Trailblazers were a group of performers who used gay tricks like fireworks and primitive pyrotechnics to put on spectacular roadside shows. After trying out some risky new material in their hit show *Mister Buffalo's Big Uh-Oh*, their audience was not pleased and demanded the Trailblazers return to the conservative, family-friendly content they had been known for. This aggravated their leader, Walter Dithney, and prompted him to write an open letter to the community where he pronounced Missouri was no longer "the vibe." He announced he would be packing up and heading west "like those two f*ggots Lewis and Clark." Shocked and excited, thousands of townsfolk scrambled to follow this courageous, brazen leader.

> "I AM DYING, I HAVE CHOLERA; MY SPOKE IS SHATTERED AND SO ARE MY DEAMS."

The trail itself was actually quite fun and included stops such as a river where you could sit and miss someone, an open field where a small group of gays collaboratively wrote *The Sound of Music*, and the first iteration of Dollywood.

We can also thank the Oregon Trail for many important historical moments. One of the earliest crossings marked the first time a gay child sat in the back seat, looked out of a window, and pretended they were in a music video. The trail also inspired the idea for the 2002 film *Crossroads*.

The influence of the Oregon Trail can still be seen today, mostly in Portland, where the visual aesthetic of the early 1800s maintains its chokehold on microbrewery and barista culture.

We cannot deny the impact of the Oregon Trail on the United States and its enduring symbolism of American grit and thirst for adventure. That being said, a lot of people died.

THE STATUE OF LIBERTY /
ELLIS ISLAND

The Statue of Liberty, originally glistening and copper-colored, became green after years of oxidation and exposure to the elements. While this fact is familiar and seems logical, it is simply untrue. The true story of the Statue of Liberty is, of course, much more gay.

In 1905, Cardinald E. Greene was one of the first people to do that thing you see in stuff like *Humans of New York*, where there is a person and everything they wear and buy for their home is the same color. It's usually older women with pink or orange or something, but in this case, it was a man, Cardinald E. Greene.

In 1908, when he came out of the period where his personal aesthetic was mostly dictated by a lot of neutral tones and funky textures, Cardinald entered a new phase where everything in his life was green. He was, of course, queer, and he would travel around to all the little shops in Manhattan buying green knick-knacks and writing little messages in green lipstick on the store windows like "Cardinald was here, queer, and Greene." He would draw a tiny picture of himself beneath the message in which he was doing the splits and holding up the words.

He quickly became one of the city's most interesting and charismatic celebrities and, by 1909, was invited by Congress to live in a little studio apartment inside the Statue of Liberty's torch. He initially refused because of the statue's color, but Congress called him— all of them at once on speakerphone—and worked out a deal wherein Cardinald would be allowed to paint the statue green temporarily, so long as he agreed to power-wash it off afterward.

A month into living in the torch, Cardinald threw a party and was smoking a cigarette near one of the open windows of the torch, when he announced, "I'm so blue I could die," slipped, and fell to his death. I know what you're thinking and, yes, *Sex and the City* stole this historical event for a cheap plot point. The Greene estate has been pursuing legal action against Darren Star since the episode aired.

Because Cardinald was the only person given clearance to power-wash the statue, it has never been done and the green paint has remained. Many have applied for permission from Congress to power-wash it themselves, as it would be a great opportunity to film the process for one of those "oddly satisfying" TikTok videos, but out of respect for Greene's memory, Congress has declined all applicants.

ATLANTIS

Hidden on the ocean floor lies the lost city of Atlantis. Theories about this ancient city range from Greek folklore about the gods smiting a prideful island all the way to a before-its-time ancient inspiration for landlocked Reno, NV, where Atlantis has become a confusing theme for a hotel/casino.

Many believe the real Atlantis was a small island that was swallowed by the sea in a natural disaster of some sort. What we know today is that Atlantis has, in fact, always been an underwater Mecca for dolphins. What we also understand today is that all dolphins are gay. Another thing we understand is that Atlantis is like the "Fire Island of the Ocean." One other thing we understand is that "it makes sense when you think about it because both of those places are super gay." These observations are attributed to Dr. Anthony [don't pronounce the H] Peabody, from the documentary *My Encounter with a Dolphin at Fire Island, Which I've Heard Is Similar to Atlantis, The Fire Island of the Ocean.*

Scientists have since learned that the seafloor of the Bermuda Triangle actually holds the entire city of **Atlantis**. The eerie tales from the Bermuda Triangle of missing ships and downed planes stem from a simple source: dolphins will target "straight idiots" (their words) flying planes and cruising ships over their city during the month of their Fringe Festival. Dolphins are notoriously cool and chill but will sink boats and use human bodies as fertilizer if you interrupt their experimental theater. But how could we possibly know all of this?

This brings us back to the documentary, *My Encounter with a Dolphin at Fire Island, Which I've Heard Is Similar to Atlantis, The Fire Island of the Ocean.* In the film, a young gay man comes to the aide of an injured dolphin who promises to share the secrets of the dolphin community in

ANDY COHEN'S GAY DOLPHIN BRAIN HAS CREATED SOME OF THE GREATEST TELEVISION OF THE TWENTY-FIRST CENTURY

exchange for help. But instead of keeping his promise, the dolphin infiltrates the young man's mind and *Freaky Friday*'s him. This dolphin man has gone on to manipulate some of the wealthiest and most influential women on the planet via a television network known as Bravo. This man? Andy Cohen. Andy Cohen's gay dolphin brain has created some of the greatest television of the twenty-first century, but the question remains: is it ethical to allow a dolphin inside of a man's body to wield so much power?

Little is known about Andy's connection to Atlantis, but what we do know is that twice a year he takes a boat to the middle of the Bermuda Triangle loaded with tons of fish and used iPhones, which he drops, sealed, into the ocean.

HOUSING MARKET

THE COLD WAR

The Iron Curtain. A time of great divide. Tension so thick the stars were blind. We are, of course, referring to the Cold War.

Often regarded as the second-most upsetting thing in American history following the 2019 Fox television special, *Rent: Live*, the Cold War shocked the world and forced the nation to ask the question: "What the hell is even that?"

The Cold War began with a large bomb in New York City on Saturday, February 5th, 2005, when Paris Hilton hosted *Saturday Night Live*, during which Nicole Richie infamously held a viewing soirée (a soirée is a gay party) for her best friend's comedic debut. This is where our war begins. According to researchers/hearsay, Nicole screened more than just Miss Lorne's Late-Night Hoohas that evening. Allegedly, she screened Paris's notorious sex tape as well. This launched the iciest feud in American history. Life . . . was no longer so simple.

America was on the hunt for answers and, like the Bush administration, both Paris and Nicole were giving us absolutely nothing. With Paris giving statements like, "It's no big secret that Nicole and I are no longer friends," and, "She knows what she did," the nation was tense and confused, which prompted Nicole to come out with strong retorts like, "Get over it," and, "We just grew apart." By this point, America needed to buy homes. That's right. They needed to buy homes where they could feel a sense of security and safety away from all this uncertainty. The banks understood this, and they felt for their fellow Americans. Soon, everyone was buying a house with loans that were quirky and chaotic. Loans that made them say, "That's hot," and, "Obsessed." Buying a home brought back the nostalgia of *The Simple Life: Season One*, when things were as they should be. Overspending brought a sense of comfort that our communities had been robbed of, but no one could have foreseen the consequences that would follow.

Please bear with us as the following paragraph is dense with complicated facts and expert jargon, but this information is highly necessary for context:

On September 9, 2008, the stock market crashed. It really ate shit. Banks were sort of like, "Whoa, what is going on?" Then money? It went way down, and everyone was not okay. Then the government said, "Listen y'all, I know it's real rough out there for the American people, so here's what we're gonna do: we're gonna give a bunch of money to these banks and then let them do, well, whatever. We don't know, lol."

It's only now, with the full context available in 2023, that historians have been able to show that the Cold War—the feud between Nicole Richie and Paris Hilton—caused the financial crisis of 2008. Everyone in the late aughts knew this was the case, but it was embarrassing to admit, so they blamed it on the banks and, surprisingly, Mariah Carey's 2001 debut film disaster, *Glitter*.

FERGIE'S NATIONAL ANTHEMS (300BC – NOW)

While much of her past is a mystery, what we know for certain is that Fergie has appeared in folklore, imagery, and songs across cultures, continents, and centuries. Sometimes she is depicted in heels and sometimes in flats, but it is most certainly always her. The throughline of these cultural depictions seems to be that she has, in every culture where she has appeared, performed a version of the people's anthem or core, sacred musical étude in a way that confused and delighted the population.

Sometimes called "the Siren of Skewed Sounds," "The Mysterious Woman in Joggers," or just "Stacy," she seems to have always risen to a level of prominence where she is tasked with performing a song meant to honor the people before a large audience. She inevitably always takes huge liberties with that musical number and then mysteriously disappears only to reemerge a century or so later to repeat the cycle. Fergie is the reason that "Frère Jacques" is often performed in the round. In the eighteenth century, she became synonymous with musical excellence among the French nobility. But at one performance, she hadn't practiced with her accompaniment. The band vamped for a full minute and a half as she tried to figure out when to come in. She kept starting at the wrong time, then going, "Oh, sorry. Fergie's just wakin' up!" before starting again. Eventually, the audience tried to help her by continuing to sing the song from where she had left off, but she didn't take their hint and started over again until eventually the song was inadvertently being performed in the round by the entire crowd. This was a happy accident until Fergie tried adding in a call-and-response portion that no one could do because it was in a language she seemingly invented. The startled audience gradually stopped singing "Frère Jacques" until it was just Fergie shouting unintelligible sounds at them, then pausing and looking around expectantly. When it became clear the audience was no longer onboard, Fergie asked if she could use the bathroom. Some confused members of the crowd nodded and she left, never to be seen again.

What is unique about the current incarnation of the immortal Fergie is that she hasn't disappeared following her unique take on America's national anthem at an NBA All-Stars game nearly five years ago. While she has kept a low profile, it seems that she is still in the country and has been building strength for what will inevitably be a powerful continuation of her chokehold on this millennium's pop music industry. Perhaps she enjoys us too much to leave. Perhaps she has some unfinished business in our time.

PAUL REVERE AND THE RICH HISTORY OF GAY YELLING

AHHHHHHHHHHH!

—PAUL REVERE

Sound gay? It is. Yelling has been inextricable from gayness since the dawn of time, and it's only right that we recognize and pay tribute to the incredibly rich, textured relationship between gayness and yelling.

Why do the moments we claim as "culturally gay" so often include a woman calling on every ounce of force in her diaphragm to yell gorgeously and melodically against a swelling orchestra or even a house beat? The energy and freedom behind simply yelling is and has always been gay.

When a straight man yells? This is a farce. A joke. A costume. Christian Bale yelling at that sweet lighting assistant struck such a chord culturally because we recognize that, as a straight actor, he had no business wielding a powerful and inherently gay tool like yelling. It's like seeing an infant in a grown woman's wig (which we highly recommend looking up).

When comedian Sue Perkins cries out "READY, SET, BAKE!" at the start of challenges in the early seasons of *The Great British Baking Show*, we are witnessing a master of her craft breeze through the intricate art of gay yelling with ease, flair, and vigor. She was *made* to yell these words. This delivery commands and demands respect and *this* is gay yelling: effective and impactful. Celestial, even.

Successful gay yelling is measured by energy and impact, folks. For this reason, one of the most important moments in our country's history is one where the power of gay yelling was harnessed for good. For centuries we've understood the tale of **Paul Revere** and his announcement of the impending British invasion as highly straight. What a shame that Paul never received his proper due. Revere could not have successfully impacted American history through a single yell without a deep connection between his little gay heart and his big gay voice.

Unfortunately, we don't have an audio recording of what he sounded like riding through the night calling his gay call. What we *can* do, however, is synthesize the details in the primary source documents we have and make scientifically backed assumptions about what he must have sounded like. From what audio science and contemporary historians have gathered, we know that he called out "The British are Coming" to the tune of Rihanna's "S.O.S." with a couple of actual lyrics from the song.

> *S.O.S. please*
> *Someone help me*
> *It's not healthy*
> *That the British ARE COMING!*

Upon the final line he would, of course, clap for emphasis on each word.

Now some practicalities: If this is indeed true, we know that it is likely he also then transitioned into the song "Tainted Love," from which Rihanna's track samples its primary hook. We can safely assume that after an hour or so of yelling "Tainted Love," his horse would have almost definitely joined in. The two would have certainly gotten carried away harmonizing and improvising ways to rework those lyrics to communicate the message of the British. This MUST have motivated and mobilized the early colonial militia intensely. Thank you, Paul Revere; thank you, Rihanna.

DISAMBIGUATION: Paul Revere is not PAUL from Genesis. PAUL from Genesis is the powerful gay creator of all things; Paul Revere is a loud gay guy from early American history. They are both named Paul because it is one of four names white gay men are allowed to have, along with Matt, Nick, and Sam.

MELISSA'S SISTER

The greatest unsung hero of our modern age has to be Melissa's Sister. Shrouded in mystery, this anonymous savior, under the alias "Melissa's Sister," has saved queer culture time and time again. Her good works include putting an end to the NO-H8 campaign after the release of that one Lin-Manuel Miranda photo, stopping Andrew Garfield from taking any more gay roles, producing Cher's one-woman television adaptation of *West Side Story*, and many more.

Not much is known about Melissa's Sister's childhood except that she was born in Coupon, Pennsylvania, which was the only fact given to authorities during an interview with Melissa's Sister's sister, Susan, at a Sizzler's, when Melissa's Sister was a suspect in the torching of a local courthouse after they refused to authenticate a same-sex marriage license. Susan described Melissa's Sister as a "force to be reckoned with" and "looking weird and scary like Tilda Swinton, but also like how Tilda Swinton is hot and beautiful." Susan never gave up Melissa's Sister's identity but confirmed she never understood the alias, considering her name was Susan and she was Melissa's Sister's only sister. Sadly, no one was able to gather more information about Melissa's Sister after Susan passed away in the summer of 2020 while watching that episode of *Drag Race* where Jeff Goldblum was the guest judge.

What we've been able to piece together about Melissa's Sister comes only through her courageous acts. There are plenty of theories about her true identity, like she might be Sia, or the Fiji water girl photobombing the 2019 Golden Globes red carpet, or all four Olsen sisters, but none have been proven. Whoever she may be, we thank her for her courageous acts and look forward to her quiet dismantling of the mid-century modern home design aesthetic, which we now recognize as violence.

DID YOU KNOW?

Melissa's Sister was and still is responsible for most major shifts in culture. Here are some you didn't know about:

+ Melissa's Sister was the first person to create a prank voicemail message. It hasn't been successfully executed since.
+ Melissa's Sister was the first person to realize Chris Pratt sucks.
+ Melissa's Sister invented the astrology app Co-Star.

CULTURE

IS GAY

VAN GOGH'S SEVERED EAR AND THE GAY LITTLE DELIVERY BOY

It was a cold night in France in 1888 when Van Gogh decided he needed some attention. A friend of Van's had just finished telling him that painting was "super gay" and that "he might as well sit on the Eiffel Tower" when he exploded into a fit of rage. In an effort to prove his heterosexuality, Van decided to do something absolutely "off the wall" crazy (this is where the concept and slogan for the Vans skate brand came from). Van Gogh was pacing his apartment searching for the perfect straight gesture when, out loud, he said, "What would really show people I'm straight?" This caught the attention of a gay little delivery boy who was passing by. From outside of Gogh's window, the gay delivery boy did sort of a ghost voice and said, "Cut off one of your ears. Straight men don't listen, right? So, that would be, like, really on the nose." When Van Gogh hesitated, the gay delivery boy's ghostlike voice boomed, "Hesitation is fag! Subtlety? Gay! Cutting ear off is touchdown!" This was revolutionary, considering this moment took place before the invention of American football. Van Gogh, stricken with the fear of not being perceived as straight, obliged and cut off his own ear.

The next day, the gay little delivery boy returned to Van Gogh's home to check on him, feeling slightly guilty for tricking him into cutting off his own ear but mostly feeling okay about it. When Van Gogh answered the door, the gay delivery boy handed him a croissant and said, "I was told to deliver this gay pastry to a certain fruity painter." He couldn't help himself. He had the pastry on him and was like, "This would be so funny." This, of course, sent Van Gogh into a frenzy. Van grabbed his severed ear and screamed "Do you see this, boy? This is my own ear that I just cut off! I am a straight artist! This proves it!" The delivery boy said, "Absolutely." Van then ordered the delivery boy to take his severed ear to a local brothel where it was to be displayed in the lobby with a note that said, "Ear of the notorious pussy slayer: Vincent Van Gogh." The gay little delivery boy agreed eagerly, letting Van Gogh know the entire world would know how deeply straight he was.

The delivery boy went directly to the local gay tavern, where the ear was fastened to the door where the gay men had to whisper the secret password to be allowed entrance. The ear remains there to this very day.

THE MONA LISA SMILE

A mystery the Italians refer to as "sfumato," which translates roughly to "pasta mouth," also known as the Mona Lisa Smile, is an enigma that has puzzled gay historians for ages and Julia Roberts since 2003, both parties sort of saying, "What was that all about?" What exactly was Mona Lisa smiling at? A question that, thankfully, has evolved since the notorious 1964 *LIFE* Magazine article about the painting entitled *Why is This Woman Smiling without Her Husband?*

There are many theories out there:

+ Someone was tickling her feet
+ She was remembering when she tried to pull a push door
+ She saw a really old couple being romantic at the park earlier
+ There was a sign in the studio that said, "I Make Wine Disappear . . . What's YOUR Superpower?"
+ She started a multi-level marketing scheme a few years back and it was just starting to pay off for her
+ She just came up with the concept for the film *Memento*
+ She was actually about to sneeze

While all of these are excellent theories that experts, and not two gay idiots, have come up with, they are incorrect.

What we know today, the reason Mona Lisa was smiling: the painter, Leonardo da Vinci, kept saying "fustrated" and "fustrating" instead of "frustrating" and "frustrated."

JEAN DEFOLEAU: THE PORTRAITIST WHO PAINTED FOR FREE JUST SO AT THE END HE COULD SHOW SOMEONE HOW UGLY THEY WERE

"Jean was a sassy little bitch," muttered one of his patrons at his funeral. Displayed on every square inch of the old church walls were thousands of Jean's hand-painted portraits, each one more disturbing than the last. And there lay Jean, open casket, arms extended straight forward, elbows locked, two middle fingers up, with the strings of a placard wrapped around them that read "Look at your nasty-ass self," just as he requested. Hundreds lined up to speak, which was unexpected considering how many of those same people had vowed to kill him in life.

A woman stepped up to the podium: "I came to him days before my wedding. I had seen an ad in the paper," she sniffled. "I told him it was for my wedding and not to mess this up because it was important. He smiled at me for, like, a few seconds too long—it was unsettling—and then said, 'Absolutely, girlie.'"

She pointed to one of the portraits on the wall. A portrait of a woman holding a bouquet of cocks smiling grotesquely in a wedding gown. Written across the gown, in what appeared to be blood, was the phrase "No one feels safe around me." On the bottom edge of the frame was a plaque that read "Look at your nasty-ass self." The woman sobbed, "He had this delivered to me on my wedding day and placed it behind me during the reception." She started to laugh, "I was mortified and livid, of course, but what shocked me was how he knew . . . how he knew that about me. None of my friends felt safe around me. Jean had such a special gift."

A voice boomed over the loudspeaker, "Look at your nasty-ass self," indicating the woman's time to speak had come to an end. It was Jean's voice. The audience smiled.

There's no doubt Jean heavily influenced the art world. His legacy includes:

+ Art majors who later went on to write for *Reductress*.
+ The idea for the restaurant Dick's Last Resort: The one where the servers are mean to you.
+ Inspiring Santa Monica Pier caricature artists. Jean did it first but was boo-ed away when he poured breadcrumbs on an older white woman who was telling him he couldn't paint there without a permit. Someone nicer liked his idea and kept the art alive.

THE TWO LESBIANS WHO CREATED ANDY WARHOL

In the year 2021, Marcia and Sarah, who had met a few months previously, moved in together, started a small business making hospital gowns for pets, and were looking to break into YouTube taste-testing videos reviewing new Trader Joe's snacks for fall. Everything was going smoothly when Sarah decided it would be fun to dump all the snacks into one bowl. Trader Joe had never allowed his products to Chex-Mix like this, understanding the potential ramifications. More often than we know, companies will risk the wellbeing of consumers by pushing known volatile products to the market, like when Interscope Records releases a DaBaby album—and this was no different. The result of combining these Trader Joe's seasonal snack items created a wormhole, tearing through the fabric of time and space. In the video, which has since been removed from YouTube, you can see not only the creation of the wormhole but also footage of a delicate-looking man mysteriously appearing in the chaos. Confused and terrified, the man is then sucked into the wormhole clutching a tote bag, which he takes with him into the unknown. Marcia screams, "My soup! He took all my Campbell's soup!" while Sarah says, "What a random wormhole!"

Transcription from the now-deleted YouTube video:

> **Marcia:** "Randy wormhole?"
> **Sarah:** "Randy Warhole."
> **Marcia:** "Randy Warhol, that's what we'll call that guy who seems to have been created by the tearing of the fabric of space and time right before our eyes."
> **Sarah:** "Randy is the name of my uncle and he's kind of a dick. Let's call him . . . Andy Warhol."

And that is how Andy Warhol was created and instantly thrust back in time. Scientists believe that combining all the unique Trader Joe's snacks created a critical mass of eclectic white energy the world hadn't seen before or since February 2019, when sixteen bisexual women started *The Artist's Way* at the exact same moment the show *Russian Doll* premiered on Netflix.

"How come I didn't hear about this?" You may be asking yourself. Well, can you just chill for one second? You're always like "Prove it, you're lying," and it's like, "Learn to trust people, you're broken." Sorry to do this right now, but we're at our breaking point. Andy Warhol WAS created in a wormhole created by two lesbians who mixed a bunch of autumnal Trader Joe's snacks together and you're going to have to take our word for it. We're not doing this again with you.

PAINTING WAR SCENES IS GAY

A young queer boy majoring in animation at CalArts sat down for his first day of class and was asked to paint the battle of the Alamo. Naturally, he was confused and tweeted "lol my art professor glorifying war on the first day of class is simply NOT the vibe." Seconds later, his tweet appeared on the projector screen behind the professor. She said to herself, loud enough for the room to hear, "Simply not the vibe . . . hmm . . ." The next slide on the projector was a photo of Marina Abramovic sitting across from the professor with a gun on the table between them. The next slide said: "Whoops, how did that get in there?" The next slide: A photo of John Trumbull's masterpiece *The Death of General Warren at the Battle of Bunker's Hill, June 17, 1775*, an emotional, jarring depiction of Joseph Warren's death during the Revolutionary War in 1775. The entire class wept. The professor stood up and said, "That's what I thought," and left the classroom. The boy who tweeted learned a valuable lesson that day: don't be such a little bitch about stuff because you're what? Nineteen? I know Marina Abramovic personally. This is, of course, what the professor emailed the student later that night.

> "YOU CAN PAINT A WAR SCENE, OR YOU CAN MAKE A SOLO SHOW."
>
> —CARL JUNG ON PROCESSING TRAUMA IN A GAY WAY

Painting war scenes has never been about war. It's been about someone (gay) holding a tiny brush (also gay) and making art out of trauma (the gayest thing you can do) so they don't have to actually fight in a war.

This awe-inspiring form of queer expression has been obscured by years of heterosexual appropriation. A gay man would paint a gay little painting of the war and a straight general would *lose their mind* praising the gay man, which fueled more war paintings for attention. Who could blame these artists for leaning into it? Imagine the power of knowing all these violent straight men were hanging your very gay art up in their homes. It's important to understand the art form's true origins so that it is not categorized with other heterosexual artistic expressions. In fact, many art historians have referred to painting war scenes as the exact artistic opposite of the *Fast & Furious* franchise.

The impulse to take something brutish and make it beautiful is drag; therefore, a painting of war is war in drag. Civil War re-enactments are nothing more than DragCon. If you're not tipping the war paintings at a museum or the Civil War re-enactors in an open field, it's considered quite rude. And if you still don't believe painting war scenes is gay, consider this: Tom of Finland is a famous "war scene" illustrator. And finally, you have to paint a shit ton of horses when you're depicting a war scene and drawing/painting horses is one of the gayest things you can do.

History Nerd @paintingwarscenesisgay
Lol this student in my class doesn't realize I saw his tweet. I'm about to pop off

Kurt @arth03
My art professor glorifying war on the first day of school is simply NOT the vibe.

Open Field.
The term **open field** refers to a piece of undeveloped land where anything is possible. Scientists have observed particles collecting in open fields in order to be gay (ponder, run toward each other, envision what *could* be). Stonehenge is actually considered an **open field** because of how gay it is.

BANKSY AND THE POWER OF QUEER ANONYMITY

You are likely familiar with English street artist, activist, and documentarian Banksy. His works have gained global notoriety for their mysterious and covert installations as well as their politically charged nature. While stealth and queerness are inarguably linked, what most solidified Banksy's position in queer art history is the anonymity of Banksy himself.

At first glance, it would be simple enough to peer through our gay magnifying glass and only explore the gayness of Banksy due to his being a well-known mononym. Mononymous celebrities are one of the purest gay cultural institutions. When we think of Madonna, Cher, or Wolverine we are immediately reminded, through their single name, of their undeniable gay adjacency. The gay nature of mononyms is mostly rooted in a rejection of the **heterosexual surname initial complex**. We see this complex most clearly in reality programs like ABC's *The Bachelor*. A community that has both a Chris S. and Chris M. operates within the strictly unimaginative confines of a straight system that ignores the social nuances that allow a gay person to know which Chris, or Hannah for that matter, is being discussed without a need to clarify through identifying their last initial. The rich tradition of adopting mononyms, not just by members of our small, local communities, but also by many of our music and film icons, has inspired and strengthened our lightning-fast gay discourse (see p. 49 and 68).

So, while his mononymous nature is queer, Banksy's anonymity is his most powerful link to queer governing concepts. There are few things queerer than disappearing into and reappearing from the ether, silent and nameless. Banksy has kept his face and true identity hidden. He's operated, more or less, as a living faceless Grindr profile for decades. Banksy is, energetically, tapping his foot in the stall next to us, and for that we must acknowledge his positioning as, at the very least, gay-adjacent.

Banksy as an entity is fully disconnected from the artist's actual identity and, in that way, we digest Banksy as more of a feeling than a person. It is fully within reason to wake up and communicate to your gay lover that you woke up feeling "a bit Banksy." Or to start a concert by calling out to the crowd, "Who here is Banksy tonight!??" to which much of the crowd would respond with a powerful cheer of affirmation. When the CW inevitably does an updated, dark television adaptation of *Austin Powers* with a hot teen cast, we can safely assume one thing: Troye Sivan, clad in a frilly lace cravat and little else as a moody, twink Austin, will inquire, "Do I make you Banksy, baby?" at some point and it will catch on.

BANKSY??

Online now

100 feet away

Tapped you 1 hour ago

The mask stays on. Not looking for anything serious.

SCULPTURE AND THE GAYNESS OF HAVING A PHYSICAL FORM AT ALL

Imagine PAUL sculpting the first man in his image, his hands smoothing out his new Earth's clay over the rippling body of what would be the Earth's first man. We aren't experts but that sounds very gay. No. Sorry. We *are* experts—that is actually the conceit of this entire book. That is gay. What PAUL did there was gay.

Since the dawn of creation, sculpting has allowed artists to bring to three-dimensional life what had previously been merely a concept and a raw material. The common understanding of sculpture is certainly more limited than the art form's actual scope. The pool of sweat that forms on a recent L.A. transplant's mat in a yoga class as she struggles in crow pose next to *Glee*'s Dianna Agron? That is a sculpture. A trail of crumpled divorce papers leading to a dimly lit bedroom where a conservative senator is buckling the back of his secret boyfriend's leather koala mask? Another sculpture, and a very good one at that. Telling a story though an object or series of objects is so deeply queer. It's why everyone who was a dedicated viewer of USA's *Monk* with Tony Shalhoub in the mid-to-late aughts is gay now.

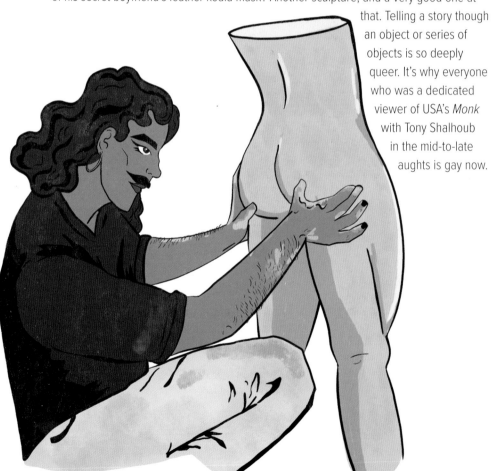

THE ALBUM ART
FOR KATY PERRY'S
TEENAGE DREAM

No existing piece of visual art holds a candle to the album art for Katy Perry's multi-platinum-selling 2010 album, *Teenage Dream*, which is universally agreed upon, in some circles, as the world's greatest work of visual art. Balance, composition, harmony: the album art is actually a 1604 oil portrait by Leonardo Da Vinci (not the famous one) and it has captured the spirits and collective hope of multiple generations spanning centuries. The pop album written to accompany this image hundreds of years later is an incredible work in itself, but nothing could speak to the masses as effectively as this painting. It is an image that says, "I have such an intimate relationship with cotton candy and its many strands that I will go on to marry two men with Hollywood's stringiest, unwashed hair just to try to keep my fervor for life alive since it remains illegal to marry the handsy anthropomorphic cloud of spun sugar I am in love with."

Scholars state that this portrait is, in fact, the actual casus belli of the Trojan War. Scholars being the name of our friend who just sort of says things. There is no evidence that this claim has any real historical legitimacy or supportive evidence.

SAYING "I LOVE WHAT YOU'VE DONE WITH THE PLACE"

The phrase "I love what you've done with the place" originated from a highly homo-erotic Shakespeare play called *The Queen's Beard*, which was banned by the Queen after a short but raucous run at The Globe. Within the story, there are two gay assassins who use the phrase as a code for when they've marked their target. A few friends who had seen the Shakespeare play decided that they would use it as a coded way to mark their own targets: people with bad taste. The friends would visit other's homes and used the phrase as a way to let the rest of the group know they did not approve of the design of the space. Most people, unaware of the very niche reference to the play, took it in earnest and were delighted, never suspecting the real meaning. So, at the end of the day, no harm no foul (which is a phrase that originally refers to chickens and is *not* a sports reference). This phrase traveled across London, eventually leading to the first-ever home renovation competition called *I Love What You've Done with the Place?,* where a very snobby gay man would travel to newly renovated Elizabethan homes and tell you whether or not he loved what you had done with the place. The winner received a modest coupon to Bed, Bath, and Beyond (many of these Elizabethan-era BB&B coupons have still not been used but continue to be redeemable).

This phrase has, however, taken on many forms and meanings since its origin. It has also been:

+ Something you have to say in front of everyone to activate an immunity idol.
+ A phrase they used in White House meetings to let everyone in the room know Kellyanne Conway was hiding under the couch to see what people were saying about her.
+ Something cheeky a villain would say after they had surprised you in your own home.
+ An awesome thing to say to your ex after not having been in their home for a few years.
+ A line of SkyMall bidets.

THE QUEEN'S BEARD

A Play by William Shakespeare

LOOKING FOR A DINNER RESERVATION FOR THE GROUP

A time-honored tradition within queer circles.

A seat at the sacred helm of queer leadership. Your community will be gathering and the fate of an entire night rests in your hands. Does the night go well, and you laugh and you cry and you share old stories from college about how insufferable Brian was before he met Stephen? Or does the service at the restaurant you choose lag, which you should've known really annoys Jeremy because he used to work in the service industry and holds every server up to the unrealistic standards to which he once held himself and now he's triggering Sam, who does *not* like when Jeremy acts like this, and Sam is the kind of person who "doesn't care and will call you out" if he doesn't like what you're doing, so now Jeremy and Sam are getting into it and Ryan is trying to make jokes to lighten the mood but none of them are really landing and Ryan isn't really used to bombing in the group, so he starts acting weird and Tom just got back from the "bathroom" where he was actually paying the check and expected to come back to the table and have everyone be like "Tom! No! Omg thank you so much!" but instead is greeted with the mess that's been created because your reservation choice was poor?

If that was stressful for you then you understand the stakes. It is a very stressful role to play. Below, we'll get into some of the qualifications and immediate disqualifications for the Reservation Seeker.

PRE-REQUISITES FOR THE RESERVATION SEEKER:

+ Successfully knowing how to order share plates for the group. Even something Derrick would like.
+ To earn basic respect, you must land at least three out of the five little jokes you're trying to tell. Otherwise, you will be categorized in a lower-level social tier like "the hot one" or "sweet."
+ You must introduce three friends to the group that everyone is "obsessed" with.
+ If you "know the chef," you have to know the chef.
+ If you actually know the chef, you are automatically qualified.

IMMEDIATE DISQUALIFICATIONS:

+ You can't have ever said, "Oh, I'm not too fussy." You actually have to be fussy; you need to be openly fussy for this.
+ You cannot be someone who prefers Starbucks.
+ You cannot be someone who meal preps.
+ If you ever refer to yourself as a foodie, you will be immediately demoted.
+ You cannot be someone who tries to make non-allergy-related modifications to your order at upscale restaurants.

This role of Reservation Seeker is not for everyone and, for those who hold the title, remember sometimes the greatest decision a leader can make is to step down and transfer power gracefully. (A close friend recently took us to a Ruth's Chris and we still haven't forgiven him).

RESERVED

"WITH GREAT
POWER
COMES GREAT
RESPONSIBILITY."
—A STRAIGHT ACTOR ACCEPTING
AN AWARD FOR A GAY ROLE

QUARTERLY MEETING OF THE HIGH GAY COUNCIL

The High Gay Council is a group of mysterious, thoroughly vetted, highly experienced gay elders who convene four times a year to decide which is the correct opinion on any and all pop-culture developments. These henceforth-correct opinions are disseminated by Twitter accounts operated by high council secretaries using computer-generated avatars of attractive, young, visibly queer **hotties**. The fake hotties signal to the community which takes are acceptable:

Date	Time		Place
Meeting Chair			
Topic	Acceptable Takes		

ATTENDEES

MEETING AGENDA

Time	Topic	Remarks
	+ Shailene Woodley's haircut	
	+ All live presentations of popular musicals aired by major television networks	
	+ Impending or recently occurred natural disasters	
	+ Who is funny right now (often it is no one)	
	+ Where in the world Carmen Sandiego is	
	+ Awards show snubs	
	+ Which non-dairy milks are trending	

The High Gay Council also decides which things are and are not gay. These proclamations are shared with the outside world exclusively via vibes. At the time of this textbook's development, the Council has issued a vibe telling us that this book is gay. It is, however, important to consider that as with all things, this could abruptly change, and the decree could be revoked at any time. This has happened with cultural phenomena like enjoying Lizzo, wearing bold patterns, calling your lover your "partner," and the *Drag Race* franchise.

The High Gay Council meets on the uncharted plot of land upon which the board for Candyland is based. Aspiring members to the Council go through a real-life set of trials based on Candyland's gameplay. Many enter the trials with high hopes of being initiated into the exclusive ranks of the Council members, but around 95 percent fail and are delegated to roles serving the High Council's more administrative needs, like researching and subscribing to the near-hourly releases of new streaming services on the Council's behalf.

FRACKING

Fracking, a destructive method of drilling for oil, is the opposite of being gay: something conservatives support but is objectively wrong.

The act of fracking was never intended to be a gay tradition and we are tied to it by name only. The name of the operation came from the son of a famous oil tycoon named Charles BigMcRich. Charles had three boys. Two of them he was proud of and the third was a big vest guy. His name was Frackson, and he was really into his cane and top hat. He wanted a mustache but couldn't grow one. He was a man with an intense personality, way too into Edgar Allen Poe. When he was younger, he was the kind of you kid you didn't feel bad being mean to. You know the ones . . . there's no fixing that. As he aged, he gained a reputation for being quite troublesome.

In 1947, the BigMcRiches invented a new method of drilling for oil. One of the oil field's neighbors was very upset about the new drilling practice and confronted Charles at a soiree, calling the new method dangerous, unethical, and disturbing, to which Charles replied, "Are you talking about the drilling or my son Frackson?" and then he looked around like he was looking for an audience to take in his joke. The local concerned man had to just stand there and wait for him to stop, dumbfounded at what money and power can do to a person. Charles turned and walked away feeling like he had said something really awesome. He began to tell the story over and over to colleagues and employees, who were too afraid to tell him it wasn't funny.

Soon the story gained infamy throughout the company, and the new drilling practice was officially referred to as Frack-ing. Frackson heard of the news and, excited to finally gain his father's approval, ran to his mother to celebrate the incredible development. She couldn't bear to let him down—although he was entirely insufferable, he was still her son. Later that night, Frackson was lying in bed thinking about what to masturbate to when a note slipped under his door in handwriting he didn't recognize. He opened it.

Dearest Frackson,

I hate to break the news about why the successful new drilling practice is named after you, but I think it's for the best. I'm going to tell you why they decided to call it Fracking: You see, you have a reputation around town for inserting yourself into places you don't belong (i.e., a conversation) and fracturing the internal mass of the structure (socially) while expelling an excess of toxicity (playing devil's advocate in a really annoying way) in order to extract resources (any attention you can get), which, ultimately, makes you very bad for the environment (party). I know this is a lot to take in and it's right around masturbation hour, but I believe the truth will set you free.

Frackson was devastated. Not only because of the letter but also because he was *just* about to choose between The Idea of Scaring Someone and An Old Man Falling for masturbation hour (he's nasty, don't feel too bad for him). Frackson was a weirdo, no doubt, but he was still a person, and this really shook him to his core.

He stopped going to family events, stopped speaking to his entire family, even his mother, and locked himself away in his room. The only person he had contact with was his butler, a tall, striking man who was around the same age as him. They became quite close. Frackson's kink was getting close to someone who was being paid to be there, and the butler was a bit of a hot idiot, so he thought most of the strange things Fracky said were jokes. As they grew closer and closer, Frackson began to soften, having finally received the steady flow of attention and admiration he'd always craved. To cut to the chase, one night they both leaned down to pick up a chip off the ground, stared at each other, then kissed. It was awesome. They spent the night entangled and Frackson awoke a new man, feeling free from the shackles of his past. The two of them ran away together, madly in love. It wasn't until they were well in their eighties that the butler revealed that it was him, so many years ago, who had written the letter telling Fracky of the truth. The two of them died in such a gay way: car accident.

This touching story is why Fracking is our tradition. Not Fracking as in drilling, but Fracking: the act of getting close with a male friend and unwittingly stumbling into gay physical intimacy. Fracking, in its true meaning, is actually just the sex that fracks you out of the closet.

MINIMALISM AND THE QUEER POWER OF BEING WITHHOLDING

Minimalism, not only in fine art but all mediums of expression, carries a great deal of queer power because of its link to the timeless queer tradition of being withholding to assert dominance. We could fill a lengthy chapter with incredible and useful details about this topic. But we won't.

WANTING TO BE A GOOD SINGER

First and foremost, singing gets you attention.

Second, it is a safety precaution. Don't want to get lost in a large crowd? Be good at singing. People will stop talking and listen to you.

Third, it's a defense mechanism. You can be good at singing, have a terrible personality, and people will still be nice to you.

Also, you can say something tacky earnestly and people won't roll their eyes at it.

And last, we must continue to sing, or an ancient beast will devour the earth.

This brings us to Simon Cowell. Simon Cowell is a 3,469-year-old dark eternal being. Born before Jesus, Simon Cowell has had a strong hold on organized singing competitions around the world for literal centuries. Our first recorded singing competition took place in ancient Egypt, when cats were first starting to rule over queer people. Simon was a kind, softhearted child. He was merely a teenager when he gathered his first group of tomb-raiders (hot gay women) to see who could scream better. Little did he know, singing had already been invented in the prehistoric era but had been lost after a group of "alternative" cavemen were asked to quiet down one night and took their coveted art form to the top of a mountain and never came back (historians now understand this is where yodeling came from).

The competition was a huge success, critics were calling it 𓀀 𓀁 𓋴 and 𓀂 𓀃. Things were going great for Simon. The competition had attracted the attention of the Pharaoh, who declared it the most important thing the Egyptians would be remembered for. Simon had climbed his way into the inner circle of elites (almost impenetrable at the time). He was an overnight celebrity and was applauded for his positive attitude and overwhelming kindness; however, he was becoming quite powerful, and it wasn't long before he pissed off the wrong people.

After a round of auditions where he denied a high-status woman a spot in the competition, he was attacked. The family of the woman did quite a number on him. He was laying in the sand, blood pouring out of him, sun in his eyes, when a hooded figured stepped into his blurring vision. The figure offered him eternal life in exchange for his soul. Simon, desperate to return to his life, agreed.

He awoke in his bed within the palace surrounded by nurses. It was a "miracle." But Simon was different. He began scowling and criticizing how the nurses in the room were standing, calling it "awkward" and "uncomfortable to look at." He resumed auditions the next day, where he called an eight-year-old girl a "sperm that should've been swallowed." Crowds were furious with him. Some started coming to the shows just to boo him. The Pharaoh was considering cancelling the competition until he realized they were making almost double the amount they had last year in ticket sales. The crowds loved to hate Simon. So, the Pharaoh encouraged him, saying the royals loved his sassy little attitude.

After this rebranding, Simon felt that he was too big for Egypt, too big for the competition, and took off into the desert night. Many believed him to be dead, and so the legend of Simon Cowell became lore after no one had seen him for years and years. Some questioned whether they had ever seen him in the first place.

Simon has made his mark all over the world throughout human history. Many believe him to be Shakespeare. We now know he was the inspiration for the hit musical *Sweeney Todd: The Demon Barber of Fleet Street*, because he actually did everything that's depicted in that musical. He has returned to his roots in our lifetime, making aspiring singers cry in front of large crowds, but will no doubt disappear into the desert night again only to emerge when the next endeavor calls to him.

CAKES THAT LOOK LIKE OTHER THINGS

In the first episode of the second season of *RuPaul's Drag Race: All Stars*, Tatianna repeats a call-and-response refrain with her audience. She challenges the notion that our reality, as we perceive it, is capable of being trusted. Back and forth, the performer and audience volley "What you see isn't always the truth." In the days following, cakes disguised as other common foods and objects overwhelmed the social media landscape. Experts tell us this was no coincidence.

The pandemic was the final push that the cakes-doing-drag corner of the internet needed to really step into the spotlight, culturally. The world rapidly became obsessed with edible delicacies realistically disguised as everyday objects. The art of illusion has been passed down through queer oral tradition for centuries and appears in many forms across historical periods. It has even penetrated the plots of some of our preeminent cultural stories and myths. Mystique from *X-Men*'s power, when you really think about it, is queerness. While many heterosexual magicians have flooded and arguably dominated the field in the past few decades, the art form at its core is rooted in queerness, as is any act of performative transformation or metamorphosis. While any particular magician today may not *be* gay, the thing he or she *is doing* is certainly gay. The gay energy released through the art of illusion does tend to skew the way the heterosexual magician presents, dresses, and behaves, transfiguring into a chimera-like abomination of the gay impulse. This is the unfortunate origin of the **steampunk aesthetic**.

Illusion—when done correctly—is pure, virtuous queer excellence. A cake masquerading as a giant cheeseburger might as well be singing a hymn to PAUL in four-part harmony. The cake is using disguise (illusion, drag, etc.) to reveal a part of itself that it may not have felt comfortable sharing prior. Maybe the cake has a hard time connecting to others because of a strained relationship with its father, but it is able to come out of its shell and feel—if only for a moment—like the life of the party when its top and bottom layers look a bit more like glistening, doughy buns. This is an important piece of context to understand as the cake tries to heal and grow. This is beautiful and honorable. Cakes that look like other things allow us to see, in high definition, how powerful and gay it is to keep something as your own sweet little secret. If you are in a classroom right now, which seems likely given that this is a textbook, look at the person sitting to your right. Now, look at the person sitting to your left. Statistically, it is more than likely that one of them is cake and all three of you are gay.

ALL CAKED UP

ANNABELLE'S REAL CURSE: IDOLS, TRINKETS, AND TCHOTCHKES

An ancient cave-witch named Annabelle had a gay neighbor who left a *Buffy the Vampire Slayer* refrigerator magnet on the post of a fence dividing their two yards. She cursed the community to an eternity of fixation upon their tiny little belongings so this would never happen again. Since then, queer people have obsessively cultivated and celebrated small, beautiful things. Early, cave-dwelling queers would often assemble small doll-like versions of the best singers of their time and place them at the entrances of their caves to let any potential visitors know what kind of house they were about to enter. This was to avoid any potential conflicts or disagreements, as fans of these prehistoric singers would fight tooth and nail to defend the honor of their icons.

It wasn't long before this practice expanded to include small tokens or trinkets that represented not only people but ideas. A queer home could be littered with small idols representing their values. Ornate candle holders and wick trimmers, a deck of playing cards with flirty little cocktail recipes on each one, napkin rings made of silicone mysteriously kept in the drawer of a bedroom side table. The values of a gay home were made evident by the small treasures its residents kept and doted upon.

AirPods, while available to straight consumers, are an invention targeted at gays, with the understanding that something so tiny and so valuable, made to go inside the ear, would be irresistible to a community that often self-soothes with new piercings or bodily adornments in times of duress. Like moths to a flame, queer people descended upon AirPods on their initial release. Today, a majority of the gay community are able to unify around the shared trauma of losing one AirPod mere weeks after purchasing. It is a testament to queer resilience that the community has persisted and is in some ways stronger than ever after the pain of **the great queer single airpod exodus of 2018.**

> "WE NEED FUN LITTLE OBJECTS. WE NEED THEM OR ELSE."
>
> —GAY ICON RONALD MCDONALD

Tchotchke.
A yiddish word that means "faggy little toy."

GOING FAST IN GENERAL

The straight community has long considered acting, speaking, or thinking quickly to be both inconvenient and avoidable. Agility and efficiency, for them, is reserved for either skipping rocks with their pal Clark or hasty rejection of any intrusive thoughts about Clark looking incredible in his new navy board shorts.

For queer people, working or playing at high speeds has been so pervasive as a tradition that it has integrated seamlessly into the fabric of queerness itself. If you are, by some cruel twist of fate, a straight person reading this book, consider that by the time you've reached this section, a queer person who started reading simultaneously next to you will have already finished the book in its entirety and moved on to integrating some of the fantastic concepts explored here into their rich, full, gorgeous life. Even a queer person whose reading skills are hampered by something like dyslexia will have sought out and found the resources or support they need to finish this book, written a powerful and moving letter to the late Princess Diana to place upon her grave, and assembled a team of misfits to uncover a political scandal by the time you've reached this chapter.

Many cultural traditions have mysterious origins that are difficult, if not impossible, to trace back to their originators. Not this one, though. In the thirteenth century, a peasant named **Walter the Scurrier** was observed by his neighbors tending to his crops at what they claimed was a delightfully homosexual speed. So delightful that a nearby lord soon got wind of Walter's gay scurry. Not to be outdone, the lord began adopting a rapid-fire gay affect in both his speech and mannerisms. Some recounted that his speech was "deliciously difficult to understand," and that he would sprint through the rooms of his manor, making little unintelligible comments to the great entertainment of his guests. Soon, this behavior had spread through the more self-identified "interesting" members of the elite class and trickled down to every person who believed they had a little something special going on.

Now, we can trace the lines backward in time from each instance of a queer speed-walking, driving-45mph-through-a-residential-neighborhood, or literally anything that Billy Eichner does, back to the 1200s, Walter, and his unforgettable contribution to this cultural tradition.

QUIZ

Test your knowledge and content retention! If you've been reading this text chronologically and paying attention, you should be able to easily answer these simple questions.

1. Do we, as humans, truly have free will?

_____

_____

_____

_____

2. Are our personalities (circle one)

the result of our environment

inherent soul-based traits

3. What is the cure for cancer?

_____

_____

_____

_____

4. What did Monica mean when she said that thing to me about my hair?

_____

_____

_____

_____

5. How do I breathe without you? I. Want. To. Know!

_____

_____

_____

_____

SECRET GAY HOLIDAYS

As with most things, gay people excel at celebrating holidays far beyond what their straight counterparts are capable of. In 1972, a general sense of restlessness in the community came to a head and the High Council instituted several additional holidays that could satisfy queer people's continuous quest for excellence in scheduled celebrations. Information about these events was to be withheld from straights to activate an additional prime gay thrill: juicy little **secrets**. If you are straight, please do not read the below. We will get in so much trouble.

Those holidays included:

+ Reverse Nude Figure Drawing Day (the person being drawn is clothed and all the artists are nude)
+ Palindrome Bonanza Weekend
+ Melissa's Sister Day
+ Revenge-Giving

+ Halloween II
+ Halloween II 2
+ Halloween III: Season of the Witch
+ Amy Adams's birthday
+ The Gay Thing that Happened at that Hockey Game Month
+ The Toni Awards (all for Toni Collette)
+ Everyone is the Same Height Today

6FT

JEFF PROBST

Jeff Probst, a 20-year-old student at NYU Tisch in the Experimental Theater wing, was working on a performance art piece for his junior thesis (a junior thesis isn't a thing, but they do it at NYU to "stand out." See p. 94). Jeff debuted his piece at a performance spa, which was described as "an open mic for queers" by a tourist who had wandered in after accepting a flyer from a group of NYU students busking in Times Square.

The performance art piece went as follows:

Jeff would enter spitting out wads of dollar bills he had shoved in his mouth. After all twenty-seven bills (representing the twenty-seven amendments passed by Congress) were spit out, he would say "CAPITAL GAINS HAVE NO NUTRITIONAL VALUE" over and over for five minutes as a commentary on endurance. At the five-minute mark, an alarm would go off and the *Survivor* theme song would play (and this was before it was the *Survivor* theme song, so at the time it was just really intense tribal music that Jeff would mime vague war gestures to—it was offensive). He would then grab three audience members and make them play a game. Whoever won the game had to cut open a pig carcass that had been stuffed with more money.

Jeff said that the piece was meant to represent "America" and "money" and "war" and "how all of those things are kinda bad if you think about it." He was not asked to present the piece at the college's Fringe Festival later that fall.

HEROES

Feeling struck down and jaded by the cutthroat nature of the experimental theater community in New York City, Jeff decided to drop out of college and move to L.A., where he felt that people wouldn't "ask so many questions about art." By his third day in the city of angels, twenty-three different strangers had pitched a television idea to him within the first five minutes of their conversation. Jeff felt the sting of relentless ambition and the fear that drives it: He was going to have to write a pilot if he was going to make it in this town. Reinvigorated by this rush of strange Hollywoodian energy, Jeff had the idea that would give his recent failure a new form. In just a matter of days, he took his performance art piece and shaped it into the concept for a show he called *Survivor.*

After many, many drafts, Jeff had something he was proud of. It was a scripted dark comedy set on a deserted island where a small group of coal miners had volunteered to play a game for a large cash prize. Everyone hated it, saying, "So, what? None of these dudes are gonna fuck? They're all alone on an island!" Jeff was devastated and abandoned the idea. It wasn't until years later that the script wound up in the hands of a hungry young CBS development executive. *She* loved it. The scrappy CBS employee pitched the idea that they have people actually play this game and record that instead. Jeff *loved* the idea and so did the brass at CBS. The world's first season of *Survivor* would air just a year later, branded with the infamous trinity: "Outwit, Outplay, Outlast," which Jeff had stolen from a phrase used by the leads in musical theater productions at NYU as a reminder to uphold the rigid hierarchy between them and the ensemble.

Although his performance art piece was a flop, when it came time to repurpose it as a reality television pitch, Jeff found his sweet spot. He translated his original idea into one of the most invigorating games the world has ever seen, and Jeff was finally able to accomplish his goal of creating a captivating critique of a capitalistic society.

We celebrate Jeff for his success as a rebel and a disruptor, but that is not why he is a hero. What makes Jeff *our* hero is being one of the proud few who took his theater training and made money off it.

THE 300 PEOPLE WHO LIVE INSIDE TONI COLETTE

Toni Collette is one Australian woman with three hundred souls who occupy her body. Toni Collette is like the rainforest, but instead of new species we are finding new people inside of her constantly. There are three hundred confirmed people inside Toni. This discovery does, unfortunately, nullify both her Golden Globe and Primetime Emmy awards for her standout performance in *United States of Tara*, because the Academy has described the role as "kind of cheating." It's unclear whether these folks are born into Toni or if there's some sort of hiccup in the natural order and, every once in a while, someone who has passed will cross into Toni Collette instead of "the other side." Nevertheless, we have been blessed to witness what can be accomplished when a community works together (that community being the hundreds of people inside of Toni Collette).

After intense study, scientists have determined that the civilization inside of Toni is virtually utopian, each of the people within working in perfect harmony. There's a phenomenon called constant-serendipity where, for example, someone will say something like, "I could go for a chocolate croissant," and a french pastry food truck will pull up and swing open its serving window. "Rom-com—like moments are happening at an almost constant rate," says Dr. Patchen, a highly regarded Colettologist, "but not in a cheesy, annoying way. It's quite earnest and beautiful, this little world inside of Toni Collette." Since beginning his research in 2001, Dr. Patchen claims to have discovered major breakthroughs for some of humanity's deadliest diseases, a claim that was debunked in the spring of 2019 after a private investigator found that Dr. Patchen was just saying that to keep funding. Thankfully, Toni herself had made enough money by then to continue funding the research independently.

People who have worked professionally with Toni have described her presence as overwhelmingly captivating. "Oftentimes you'll see her from across the way, asking herself a question and then answering as if she wasn't the person who just asked it." On the set of *Hereditary*, she was a much-needed positive energy, because, as she explained it, she was full of people who had experienced dying and it's actually not that scary. We have so much to learn from the living wonder of the world that is Toni Collette, and we have only scratched the surface as to what's going on in there.

GRUMPY OF THE SEVEN DWARVES

Here we present to you a poem found on a napkin about Grumpy of the Seven Dwarves, written by a gay Disneyland employee who "thought this was gonna be their *Harry Potter*" in 2021:

To be grumpy is revolutionary. Grumpy may just be one of seven short gay men a white woman surrounds herself with to escape her hellish reality, but Grumpy is an ideology.

Grumpy is brave. Grumpy is a rebellion against the niceties of heteronormative culture.

Grumpy is Bernie Sanders in the 1960s. Grumpy is not AOC in her MET Gala dress. That was the idea of Grumpy. That was playing at Grumpy.

Grumpy is the epitome of the The Customer is NOT Always Right revolution.

Grumpy is the labor shortage. Grumpy is an employee's economy.

Grumpy is Garfield, Garfield is Grumpy. Grumpy did not get the same stage time. He was actually the first cartoon character to say they hated Mondays.

Grumpy is a bad haircut on a queer person.

Grumpy is the DSA.

Grumpy is the grumpy old queer we know and love. A vital archetype for the masses to witness because not everyone has an opportunity to visit Palm Springs.

Grumpy is the great balancer. Grumpy is the grounding force of our universe.

Grumpy is dark matter.

Grumpy is string theory. Chaos.

Grumpy is the astral projection of the queer experience.

WILSON
FROM *CASTAWAY*

Wilson from *Castaway* made history as the first gay person to ever be quiet. He also is an important part of the time-honored American tradition of athletes continuing to be celebrated by the public despite very obviously having blood on their hands.

Wilson spent much of his childhood underestimated and ignored due to his body type (not having one) and his tendency to keep his thoughts to himself, but he quickly committed himself to the pursuit of sport and rose through the ranks to find himself a Division One athlete at the age of four. After a myriad of tumultuous relationships with high-profile celebrities, Wilson retired to an island to escape the public eye. He re-emerged briefly and played an important role in campaigning for the repeal of the U.S. military's "Don't Ask, Don't Tell" policy with his song and companion video entitled, "Bounce That! (Troops have got to ask and tell)." Wilson had never served in the military, but nearly all his brothers had. Wilson said he wanted to make his family happy but couldn't imagine "going even one second without absolutely living out loud." After the repeal of the policy, Wilson returned to his private island and has yet to make another public appearance.

There are rumors that he could potentially emerge from his retirement to appear on an upcoming season of Ryan Murphy's *American Horror Story* as a powerful male witch who is famous for playing the drums without arms.

DID YOU KNOW?

Wilson's cousin, Spalding, won a GLAAD award for his performance in the music video for Normani's 2019 breakout single, "Motivation."

MOMS AROUND THE WORLD

Mothers are heroes. Gay people experience mothers and motherhood much more deeply than our straight counterparts. This is because we are inherently more generative, tender, and have statistically wider feet. (Do not look this up. Trust us. We are so smart.) Motherhood, in this text, does not refer specifically to the direct maternal blood relative of a subject, though that kind of mother can fall under the umbrella of mothers as they are described here.

Motherhood is the experience of tending to or nurturing the inherent seed of queerness in an individual. Mothers see the potential for a more realized, potent gay existence, and they water the seed with vigor. These mothers are connected to an ancient gay oneness that instinctually guides them toward dance studios, blogging spaces, and yearbook clubs.

Here are some examples of mothers as we see them:

+ The gust of wind that blows the silky scarf you are wearing
+ All English teachers
+ Anyone involved with making a music video
+ Little Mix
+ People talking shit about JK Rowling on podcasts
+ Ursula, Scar, Hades, etc.
+ Girls who run the dressing rooms at clothing stores
+ Obviously drag mothers
+ Best supporting actress nominees
+ The concept of Downtown
+ The paperclip from Microsoft Word
+ Anyone playing as the "healer" class in an RPG video game

All of these people, ideas, and elemental forces are moms and thus heroes. They deserve high-budget, dramatic retellings of their origin stories spread out over three two-and-a-half-hour-long films that are nearly too dark to see but have *very* loud action sequences. It's always Mother's Day. Give them their flowers!

VERY STRAIGHT VILLAINS

There are plenty of straight people, forces, and institutions that serve as villainous inhibitors to the gorgeous and full gay experience everyone has a right to. While not all are intentional or malicious, all provide some manner of restriction or inconvenience to what would otherwise be a stunning, vibrant, satisfying gay world.

- Gritty detective dramas
- The Academy
- Ronald Reagan and his legacy
- Parties that we, the authors, are not invited to
- Landlords
- Invoking PAUL to serve one's own poisonous prescriptive views on human sexuality
- Goblins
- JK Rowling
- Toilets without bidets

TWINS: ONE IS GAY, AND ONE ISN'T

When a woman is pregnant with twins, sometimes it is the case that one of the fetuses is gay and one is not. That womb is Nature's most powerful embassy. The concept of an ambassador would not exist if not for sets of twins that include both a gay and non-gay twin. Twin combinations of this kind are referred to as **cup-string sets**. This is a nod to the practice of speaking through a cup tied to a string tied to another cup that is placed against another party's ear. Often there is perceived tension between the two communities (straight and regular), which impedes real progress. Sets of twins, however, can navigate that divide because of their otherwise entirely shared histories and genetic codes. When it comes time to share the many advanced cultural and scientific findings of the gay community with the heterosexual community, the Council tasks the gay members of each of these cup-string sets with explaining these findings, often slowly and using easily digestible words, to their straight sibling. This is how straight communities finally caught wind of important gay cultural phenomena like Dua Lipa and eating ass.

The High Gay Council designates a specific and dedicated task force to ensure that these cup-string sets of twins continue to exist globally and across generations. Cup-string sets exist in Nature but with an essentially randomized frequency and location. Luckily, the Council has uncovered ways of encouraging this kind of womb development in expectant mothers of twins. One method is playing "Déjà Vu" through headphones placed on the pregnant belly and having Beyoncé's parts come through the left ear and Jay Z's come through the right. A newer method the Council has experimented with over the past few years has been offering expectant mothers discounted ASOS color-blocked jeans wherein each leg is a different wash of denim. Unfortunately, this method is still being fine-tuned. Many of the twins born to the mothers affected by the color-blocked-leg method are both coming out bisexual. Twins that are both bisexual are incredibly powerful and there is too much leadership potential within each twin for either to ever serve as merely an ambassador.

The spies from the *Spy v. Spy* comics have disclosed that they are a cup-string set of twins but will not confirm whether the gay twin is the one in white or the one in black. At the time of publishing, the High Council has experts looking into the browser histories of each, but the twins are spies so they, of course, do an unimaginably thorough job covering their tracks.

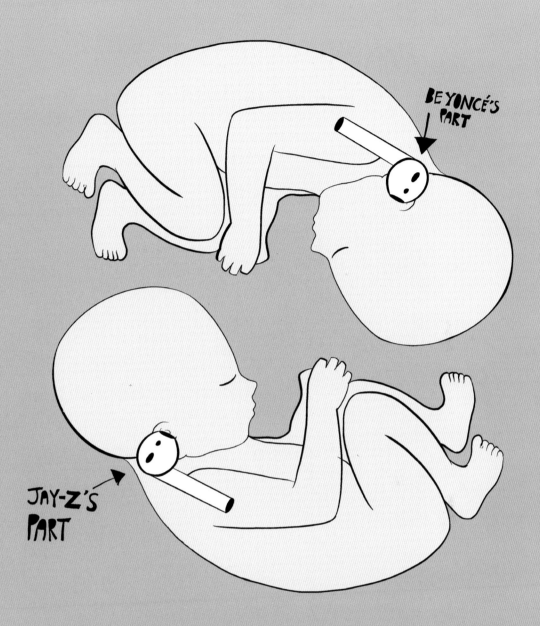

BEYONCÉ'S PART

JAY-Z'S PART

DID YOU KNOW?

There is an arrow in the negative space between the E and the X in the FedEx logo. This arrow is always pointing forward, in the direction the truck is going. This is to mimic that thing that drag queens will do where they point in the direction they're about to walk on the runway. Fed Ex stands for Federicka Excellence from the legendary House of Excellence, and she always has a special delivery for YOU, DARLING!!!

THE OTHER STONEWALL JACKSON

Many hear the name "Stonewall Jackson" and immediately think of the Confederate general mysteriously celebrated in some parts of the United States despite fighting and badly losing a war in the name of a despicable, inhuman ideology. For the purposes of our study, we focus in this text on a different Stonewall Jackson, who was superior in both moral character and general vibe.

Stonewall Jackson was a gay little parrot who lived in the attic of the Stonewall Inn during the late 1960s and served as a sort of exotic carrier pigeon for the staff, regulars, and members of New York City's queer elite. Jackson would join the bar's tipping pool on any given night to carry simple messages, complicated messages, and occasionally messages that could only be communicated physically. For a time, he delivered the iconic Warhol wigs from Andy to his lookalikes when they would speak at events that Warhol did not want to attend himself. New Yorkers from the time recall seeing what looked like a small white shih tzu flying over midtown Manhattan, which would later be revealed in Jackson's memoirs as him delivering yet another Warhol wig. Once Jackson himself posed as Andy and delivered one of Warhol's speeches to a group of students at Columbia. The students shared that they had never been so moved by a speech and that the words seemed to "wash over them as if spoken by a celestial voice within." Warhol declined to use Jackson again after that because Jackson's presence was too profound and intense to mimic Warhol's more aloof and casual persona. He also refused to even mention that the graduates keep a look out, in a few decades, for the amazing autumnal snack offerings from Trader Joe's.

Jackson would also collect shiny objects and create nests that would become elaborate headdresses for many of the Drag Queens and trans women leading the gay liberation movement. Having a **"Jackson original"** became a status symbol and commanded a lot of respect within the queer community. Jackson created fifteen of these in his lifetime before moving to Bali in the seventies with a high-profile lover, whose identity he could not disclose but who, he said, "did a lot of work with loops." These fifteen Jackson originals are considered priceless relics and have been the subject of some of history's most brutal bidding wars.

THE RULES OF FOOTBALL

TOUCHDOWN

This is when a player has had too much wine and they touch the surface of the couch or chair they're about to sit on to make sure it's still there before they sit down. If they do this enough times, they get to take off their sweaty helmets for five minutes as a little treat.

50-YARD LINE

You can't cross this line if you're being a bitch. The referee will ask how you think the game's going, and if you say anything kind of bitchy, you can't cross that line for the whole game.

PENALTY

The referees will throw a yellow flag really high into the air. If they break the current height record, they get to decide who performs in the Superbowl Halftime Show that year.

HALFTIME SHOW

This is what decides the winner of the game during the Superbowl.

COIN TOSS

This is where an old wizard tells each team's captain a riddle, and if they don't solve it, they have to explain what Fantasy Football is to someone who doesn't get it.

KICK-OFF

This is where the players come out onto the field one at a time and see who can do a better job of initiating a party. It's more of an acting exercise and competition.

END ZONE

Each player pitches a new *Avengers* movie.

TIMEOUT

If a player can successfully stop time at any point during the game, they automatically win the game. This has never been done by a football player. The only person to ever stop time successfully during a football game was Janet Jackson.

OVERTIME

If at any point a player decides that they are "over it," the game must immediately end.

FUMBLE

A small elf who meddles with the game.

PIGSKIN

Another elf who is *really* into maintaining the integrity of the game. Does *not* get along with Fumble.

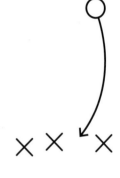

LIL' BITCH

FRINGE FESTIVAL

One of the most vicious and gay sports in human history: fringe festival. A cunning game of wit, social skills, and endurance.

Invented in 1947 in Edinburgh, Scotland, the festival started with good intentions as a way for theater kids to make their interests even more niche. The first fringe festival consisted of eight different solo shows, each titled, "When It's Never Enough." It was a blast for those involved and a disturbing experience for the bar owners who had rented out their basements to the performers. The initial group had such a great time that they vowed to make it an annual event and immediately started planning for the next year. As the next festival approached, the small team had curated what they believed to be an impeccable lineup of artists. However, after the lineup was announced, letters from friends of the festival curators began pouring in. We were able to track down one of those original letters from 1947:

Hey Samuel,

SO excited for the upcoming fringe festival!! How exciting!!! Saw the lineup. LOVED it. Obviously knew you'd do an incredible job curating. Seriously, love it lol. Are you and Sarah still butting heads? Ugh, she can really be a lot. I was just writing to say congrats and that if you need any openers for the show, you know I'm here, girl! Lol, no but seriously, would love to help in any way possible this year. As a performer. And would just DIE to be presented next year. Keep me in mind! You did say I was one of the bravest performers you've seen so . . . I'm just wondering if I had slipped your mind or something for this year. Saw you put Dina Leving on the lineup. Thought you said she was obnoxious . . .? Lol sorry. I'm just a little bummed! No worries, though. You know I won't take this personally #resilient. Okay, well, I guess that's it . . . Oh, and let me know if I've upset you in any way or anything. Obviously, you can communicate with me about anything. I know we've sort of drifted apart since I started dating Charles, but you're like super important to me and I'd love to grab lunch soon. So proud of you!! Can't wait to be on the lineup next year!!!!!!! LOLOLOL, you know I'm kiddin' ;)

XO,
Grant

Things got ugly. Relationships were destroyed, friendships were ruined—all in the span of a few months. People showed up to the festival, but, oh boy, were they talking. Suddenly some of their favorite performers' work was "getting a little stale." The spirit of competition had entered the black box theater and there was no going back. The festival, however, was a hit. At the afterparty, there was a level of schmoozing the world had never seen before. Everyone was "on," fighting for the attention of the eight curators.

A very intricate game began. At the end of the festival, a local actress's father surprised the festival curators with a $10,000 donation toward next year's events. It was a bold move that landed the actress a coveted spot in the next festival, causing an uproar through the community behind closed doors. Whispering became a huge part of the community's communication. More advanced members were even able to gossip at public events by just making eyes. A troublesome performer who went by the stage name ROCCO introduced the infamous tactic of The Rumor. This spread misinformation throughout the fringe community, ruining countless reputations, and secured ROCCO a role in one of the festival's productions until his retirement in 1972.

By the time the festival had reached its tenth year, some of the top dogs in the sport had become resident artists. Were their shows good? Almost never, but they had *huge* budgets, so they *seemed* really important. But this was the year a newcomer shook the game to its core by bringing an incredible show to the festival. Audiences couldn't stay away, and it sold out every night, with hundreds of people turned away at the door. The dull and pounding envy this shot through the community was undeniable. The newcomer was asked to come back as a resident artist the next year, something thousands of players had fought for for over a decade. This added the most valuable new element the festival had ever seen: making good art, which is truly the only way you win at the game of fringe festival.

FINISHING A CONVERSATION WITH SOMETHING QUIPPY

A fast-paced, high-risk game. Do you risk it all and try to land one final quip? It could crush, or it could fall flat, and then you have an entire room looking at you knowing that you thought you were saying something quippy but it was one too many additions to the end of a conversation.

This game was first invented by Shakespeare, who is, of course, Simon Cowell.

The game begins when a conversation is nearing a wrapping-up point and a player has an opening to make a joke or witty statement that garners a laugh before the discussion or party ends, leaving a favorable, memorable impression of the player on the group. When the opening presents itself, you don't want to move too quickly—there's a finesse to the rhythm. Too slow, though, and you'll miss your window of opportunity. Are you accounting for the energy level of the group? Don't do a bit that takes up too much space if people are tired. Get in and get out. You can be shady but not enough to do any real emotional damage. Keep it light. If you do venture into personal territory, never show your weakness. Nothing is personal. You cannot and never will be a professional player if you take this game personally.

There are immediate wins: If the group is laughing too hard at your quip and the next player tries to say something that no one hears and when you circulate for another drink someone follows you, you've scored BIG time. That's a top-ten play of the year there. People will remember and you can convert your game points into social currency.

It is, however, a dangerous game that you can't let go to your head because as soon as you do, that leaves an opening for an adversary. It's a never-ending balance; a beautiful practice of knowing oneself and the proper level of irreverence. A delight in the marriage of the sharpness of the tongue and mind.

> And tell THAT to Mister Balenciaga.

> That's what we thought until she opened her mouth.

POWERFUL WOMEN
IN SENSIBLE SHOES

One of the great triumphs of sport as an institution has been the queering of women's footwear. Many twenty-first-century sporting activities demand of their participants shoes that are sensible, functional, and durable. While there *is* plenty of space for hyper-feminization and impracticality in queer footwear, aligning a powerful woman with a sensible shoe for the purpose of athletic competition is rooted in queer necessity. In 1421, the global organization the **Queer Utilitarian Institute of Catching and Kicking** or **QUICK** determined that many female athletes were suffering physical complications from playing their respective sports in the six-inch, white platform heels that were regulation at the time.

QUICK championed a campaign led by many of the top female athletes across the globe who claimed that these shoes were, bizarrely enough, not helping their gameplay. The athletes weren't tripping or falling, as one might assume, however. They were instead struggling with how the heels made them feel like ruthless alien conquerors. Matches, with higher and higher frequency, were being called off because teams of queer women would drop their bats/balls/nets/etc. and pin their opponents to the earth with their unbelievably tall shoes. The athletes would abandon the game entirely to actually *become* legions of space conquerors. Many of these parties elected never to return to Earth. Generations of these early athletes have now had fulfilling, colorful careers as intergalactic warlords. While these games were thrilling, variety of sport is important to the Queer Utilitarian Institute of Catching and Kicking and they felt they needed to act before every women's sport devolved into a new race of female space warriors.

Before long, QUICK adjusted the standard issue footwear to the flat, comfortable athletic shoe, whose variations we are familiar with today. After this change, players found that they were able to access their sportsmanship and yield once again to the referees and the rules of their given sport. They were able to limit their role as ruthless subjugators to the field. QUICK soon realized that the sensible footwear also happened to make the physical feats of a sport simpler to execute, which opened the door to men playing sports a few decades later.

SPORTS ON THE BEACH (SOMEHOW GAYER?)

All volleyball is gay, but **beach volleyball** is gayer than indoor volleyball, and many gay academics have spent entire careers exploring the reasons why. At first, the commonly held belief was that it had to do with the sizes of the teams. There are typically two players on each team in regulation beach volleyball games, where there would be six on an indoor team. Researchers speculated that the intimacy achieved on a smaller team was what caused the readings on the devices experts use to measure gayness to spike during beach volleyball matches. The partners on beach volleyball teams have a connection more intimate and emotional than twins. Scientists have experimented with putting teammates in two separate rooms and showing one teammate a video of an elaborate flash-mob proposal and, without fail, the other would start grimacing and rolling their eyes in the next room as if they'd seen it themselves.

It wasn't long before the speculation that two-player teams were the root of increased gayness was debunked, as experts discovered that even casual beach volleyball games with many players were significantly gayer than indoor games. They also found that other sports played on the beach caused gay levels to spike in much the same way as beach volleyball. In one instance, a game of beach pool (yes, they brought a pool table to the beach—exceedingly queer) caused one of the devices to short-circuit because of how off-the-charts gay it was. This led many to the conclusion that all sports played beachside are categorically gayer than their non-beach counterparts.

So, what is it about the beach that makes playing a sport there so gay?

In the past decade, a few key findings have been uncovered that shed light on this question:

Proximity to the Ocean. The ocean is a lesbian and non-monogamously partnered with the moon. That's why, if you spend an entire day at the beach, you will notice that after interacting with you for only an afternoon, she is ready to move in.

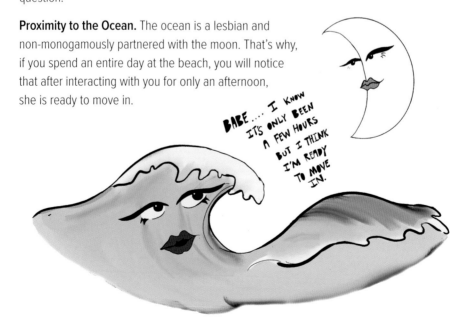

BABE.... I KNOW IT'S ONLY BEEN A FEW HOURS BUT I THINK I'M READY TO MOVE IN.

Running, Jumping, Etc., on the Beach is Much Harder. Queer people are used to things being made much more unnecessarily difficult for them. Playing in sand is so much harder than playing on stable ground. It doesn't really make sense to play sports in sand, and *that* is gay.

Sparkling Crystals of Sand Make Your Butt Crack Shimmer in the Light. Straight people have no need for/do not deserve an aesthetically delightful butt crack.

Fish are Gay and they are always singing a Charli XCX song underwater that humans cannot hear but *can* feel. *The Little Mermaid* has a nearly 100 percent accurate depiction of this, except in real life it's not "Under the Sea," it is "Vroom Vroom."

HALFTIME SHOWS

Halftime shows and performances are gay staples, but many of the reasons we, culturally, align these events with gayness are incidental and don't speak to the inherent gay nature of taking a fun little break.

It is a common queer experience to plan for a small break from a large task but then to become more involved and committed to your break activity than the original task. This is a more pervasive occurrence than one might think. Consider how involved and celebratory the second act overture of a musical is when an audience is brought back from intermission. It weaves together all the show's most iconic songs with fantastic intricacy. Often it will feel that the composer spent more time on that piece than they did making any of the individual songs. How wonderful! Consider, also, the gay impulse to stop mid-coitus to engage in a lively debate about the merits of a particular reality television program. This debate then defines the entire night. Sex is not concluded. Finally, consider, the common queer experience of eating half a sandwich, taking a break to create an elaborate short film about the stubborn but fragile matriarch of a rural family torn apart by the cruel whims of capitalism and industry, then returning to the now-humdrum sandwich. It happens all the time.

The childhood impulse to value recess above all other subjects in school is a pre-sexual queer impulse that, upon maturation, either becomes vestigial core queerness or dissipates to, sadly, toxic heterosexuality. Those individuals who retain their core queerness are to be credited for the ideation and development of the halftime show as a concept.

Halftime shows exist most prominently in sports, but they are in no way limited to that realm. TikToks are, energetically, halftime shows. So is putting on a big hat, local commercials with iconic jingles, and the many fast-food restaurants in the city of **Barstow**. If an interlude has the potential to be more exciting than whatever it is interluding, it is a halftime show. And it is gay.

DID YOU KNOW?

The official referee uniform was created in 1914 when a queer Foot Locker employee wandered into an unorganized game of basketball and took control of the situation. The Foot Locker uniforms are <u>not</u> referee uniforms.
It's the other way around.

GAY SPORTS THROUGHOUT HISTORY THAT NO LONGER EXIST

Tag: A game with two players. Both players go to each other's homes and add price tags to everything, guessing how much was paid for each item. If they get it right, they get one point. If they get it wrong but successfully defend why it should cost the amount guessed, the player gets two points. If one player offends the other player while successfully defending their guess, that player gets five points. If a player decides they don't want to play the game anymore because it's not fun, it's just mean, the other player gets ten points. If that same player says, "I don't even care if this gets you ten points, fuck this game, and fuck you," the other player gets another twenty-five points. If the player being yelled at buys that the "offended" player is actually offended, the "offended" player gets thirty-five points. If the tricked player says, "Wow, that was really manipulative," no one gets any points. If at any point a player asks the rules of the game again, that player is deducted fifty points. If at any point one of the players wants to stop the game, they have to get a temporary tattoo put on their face that says "I'm a dumb little bitch" and must continue playing the game. Once someone starts crying, the game is over and all of the points are tallied. This game was only played once in ancient Mesopotamia.

DoTerra-ing: A game where a player invents a product that they must get others to use. As the player progresses through the game's levels, they must also convince new players to join the game and help them share their product, encouraging those new players to also recruit their own new players to help share the product. Once the player has done that enough, they stop playing the game. However, if any of the players they brought into the game leave, their score goes down. If the product they invented loses popularity, then the entire structure they created will be destroyed. However, during gameplay, if the player does a bunch of supremely fucked-up shit in pursuit of more players or wider product reach, then there's the possibility for the coveted docuseries bump, where the documentary about their failure launches the player back into the public eye and gives their original product an ironic new boost, winning them the game. This game no longer exists, as MLMs have taken its place.

N.Y.C. vs. L.A.: Played mostly by residents of these two cities and any young queer person in a smaller town deciding where to move. This game no longer exists because the winning city has been decided. It's Eureka Springs, Arkansas.

Ring Around the Rosie: Everyone is constantly running circles around Rosie O'Donnell. This game is no longer played because Rosie became mean.

--- BONUS SPORT ---

Playing Masc in an Audition Room: A sport invented by Tom Cruise.

SOMETHING THAT HAPPENED ONE TIME AT A HOCKEY GAME

In March of 1991, during a hockey game, the gayest thing in recorded history happened. In the moments leading up to the event, the air became thick with a palpable queerness. Witnesses have stated that they remember the hairs on the back of their necks and on their arms sticking straight up and then bending slightly, the way people do that thing with their wrists when they say "Is he? . . . you know." News media rushed to cover the event but arrived too late. By the time they pulled into the parking lot of the rink, the gay thing that happened was over and the world would have to adjust to things feeling universally gayer from then on. World leaders had no choice but to release statements acknowledging what had happened, that it was gay, and that they had taken notice.

One of the players went on record saying, "I didn't know something this gay was possible. I know we all made jokes about something *so, SO* unbelievably gay happening during a game one day, but I never thought it actually would. Much less to us. Boy, did this shut me up."

The Zamboni driver from that day has spoken at the GLAAD Awards nearly every year since, and each year he gets about thirty seconds into his speech before he is overcome with emotion, tears up the paper on which his speech is written, and begins feebly singing what little he knows of the song "True Colors." He only knows a few of the lyrics and hasn't bothered to learn any more in the past thirty years, but the audience typically joins in to help him out.

March is observed, yearly, as The Gay Thing that Happened at the Hockey Game Month, and cities around the world have put together dazzling parades and street festivals trying to recreate even a fraction of the feeling that must have hung in the air when the gay thing that happened at that hockey game in March of 1991 happened. Twenty percent of children born to queer parents in 1992 were named Hockey Game, and the rink was renamed "Gay Thing that Happened Here Hockey Rink." It was registered as a historical landmark in December of 1992 and is visited yearly by more tourists than Jerusalem and the Eiffel Tower combined.

69 NEWS   GAY THING HAPPENED AT HOCKEY GAME
BREAKING NEWS

THE INHERENT POWER IN ELECTING NOT TO PLAY

Make no mistake, playing sports *can be* and often *is* gay. There is, however, an even gayer option available. Whether skilled or unskilled in athletics, regardless of the other players involved or of the play in question, it is extraordinarily gay to decline to participate in a sports game. Some of the gay strength present in this refusal is connected back to the queer power of being withholding, but it goes beyond that. Electing not to play a sport, especially one you've been invited to play, begs the question: What will you be doing instead? It *is* an important element of this refusal to at the very least *appear* to be immersed in a much more interesting, **"authentically-individual"** activity while sitting out. This can include wistful gazing, wordlessly rehearsing the facial expressions you'd make while giving a speech, or getting lost in a memory.

Sports generate so much collective energy from their collaborative nature, but there is a more powerful individual energetic emission created by mysteriously declining to play and then giving a vague explanation why which makes little to no sense. Other players will have no choice but to preoccupy themselves trying to sort out what exciting opportunity and individual exploration exist outside of the game and its made-up rules. Inevitably, this curiosity will broaden into the question, "What exciting opportunity and individual exploration exist outside of the made-up rules I've created in my own life and in my community?" And further, "Have I been keeping my friendship with my same-sex teammates one-dimensional and limited in its intimacy because I'm scared of the possibility that I might be perceived as or even actually *be* gay?" And, eventually, "Wow. I am gay." Then, finally, "They should make an ensemble film with all of the best supporting actress nominees of the last decade."

This *will* happen. This is the power of non-participation.

HAVING A SMOOTHIE? YOU'RE GAY.

The following is a script from a gay food safety training video.

Employee: Yes, you read that correctly. Scientists astounded the beverage world in 2021 after finally releasing thousands of peer-reviewed studies with extensive evidence that if you are having a smoothie, you are, in fact, gay.

Customer: Do protein shakes count?

Employee: Yes, those make you ultra-gay.

Customer: Is there any way to avoid this?

Employee: No.

Customer: What do I do now?

Employee: Here's what you can do: enjoy it. Enjoy your gay little life. Blend up those fruits and veggies. Add that protein powder. You've got one life to live. Are you going to let your fear of being gay stop you from drinking smoothies? Some of you probably will. Those of you who have accepted your new identity get to enjoy the freedom that comes from having a smoothie and being gay (two things we know are synonymous).

Customer: What if I am on vacation and I'm just having, like, a frozen drink?

Employee: You're gay.

Customer: Ok, what if—

Employee: Ok, what if you stopped trying to get out of this. If you are having a smoothie, you are gay. There's no way around it. A smoothie is anything blended, according to scientists.

Customer: Does that mean—

Employee: Yes, that means even if someone has blended ingredients that have gone into a soup, you are having a hot smoothie and you are gay.

Customer: . . .

Employee: Any more questions?

Customer: Nope.

Employee: Oh . . . ok . . . How are you feeling about it?

Customer: Honestly, kind of great.

Employee: Oh, wow. Ok cool. I love that. That's, that's really good.

Customer: Yeah, it's just like hey you know what: I'm having a smoothie and I'm gay!

Employee: Yeah!

Customer: I put protein in there, I'm extra-gay!

Employee: It's ultra-gay.

Customer: Ultra-gay!

Employee: Yes!

Customer: Yeah, I feel really good about this.

Employee: Great! If you could just step to the side, I do have to take the next customer's order. Hi, welcome to Jamba Juice. My name's Albert and, yes, you are reading that sign correctly: If you are having a smoothie, you are gay.

FEELING FRUITY

THE GAY SECRETS OF AMERICA'S LARGEST CHAIN RESTAURANTS

Chili's: The tortilla chips are so thin and delicate. That's gay.

Outback Steakhouse: The mountains in the logo above the text are actually the Brokeback Mountain range.

TGI Friday's: Every photo on the wall has J.Lo expertly photoshopped into it. Next time you're in there, look harder.

Olive Garden: "When you're here, you're family" means when you're there, you're chosen family, so you're gay.

Buca Di Beppo: The last bite of spaghetti at the bottom of your bowl will spell out "Hey, Soul Sister," a song about two gay friends that had sex once but then decided they were just best friends.

Applebee's: Applebees are gay bees that will only pollinate apples because they're picky.

Buffalo Wild Wings: In the bathrooms there are holes cut into the walls between the toilet stalls . . . where you can share some of your wings with a stranger because sharing is caring and caring about things is gay.

Red Lobster: Every Red Lobster is also a courthouse that can issue same-sex marriage licenses.

The Cheesecake Factory: All the cheesecakes in the case are from a cancelled gay wedding.

FOOD THAT LOOKS LIKE ACADEMY AWARD WINNERS (FEMALE-IDENTIFYING ONLY)

VIOLA DAVIS TOAST

This is Viola Davis on toast. The only other person to be seen on toast is Jesus. Something to think about. Davis won an Oscar for Best Supporting Actress in the 2016 film *Fences*.

CHARLIZE THERON BEET

In 2017, Charlize Theron famously switched places with her underground government copy (like in the movie *Us*) for a much needed reprieve. The Copy Charlize, with no cultural context, agreed to sport dreads in the 2017 film *The Fate of The Furious*, prompting Real Charlize to quickly return to the surface and the screen sporting a culturally appropriate bowl cut in the series' next installment, *F9*. It's safe to assume this beet is a message from Copy Charlize. Scientists are not quite sure what the copy is trying to tell us, but Real Charlize has assured us "it's nothing scary, so don't even think it is for one second."

MICHELLE YEOH GREEN BELL PEPPER

Michelle Yeoh is perfect and always has been. This book was written in 2022 with a vehement belief that Michelle Yeoh would win the Oscar for Best Actress in the 2022 film *Everything Everywhere All At Once*. If that didn't happen, destroy the Academy.

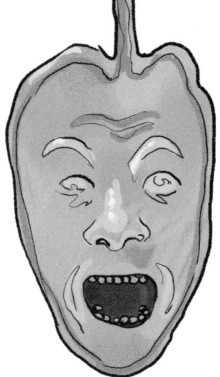

FOOD PYRAMID
FOR GAY PEOPLE

COMBINATION MEALS: BRUNCH, LINNER, DINFAST

Much like the Banach-Tarski Paradox, the sum of the meals is greater than their parts.
The fact that the meal period is combined is more important fuel for the body than
whatever the actual meal consists of.

GARNISHES

A necessary element of not just cocktails but any beverage.
For gay people, visual interest is as essential as the mineral iron.

**EITHER CARBOHYDRATES OR EXPLAINING WHAT KETO IS
(you can choose)**

Choose one.

CAFFEINE

It's actually important to push back on what the
body communicates as its limits here. This is one
of the few instances when your body doesn't know
what's best for you and you should have more
than you think you need.

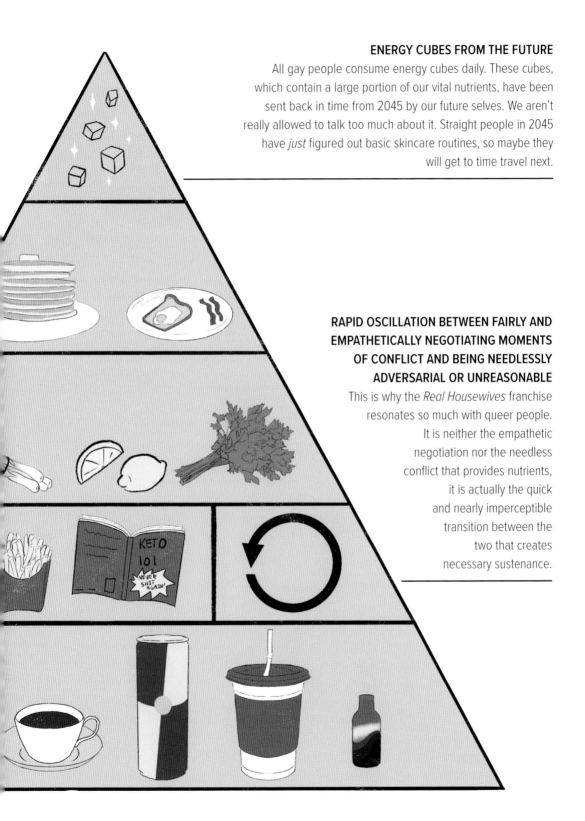

ENERGY CUBES FROM THE FUTURE

All gay people consume energy cubes daily. These cubes, which contain a large portion of our vital nutrients, have been sent back in time from 2045 by our future selves. We aren't really allowed to talk too much about it. Straight people in 2045 have *just* figured out basic skincare routines, so maybe they will get to time travel next.

RAPID OSCILLATION BETWEEN FAIRLY AND EMPATHETICALLY NEGOTIATING MOMENTS OF CONFLICT AND BEING NEEDLESSLY ADVERSARIAL OR UNREASONABLE

This is why the *Real Housewives* franchise resonates so much with queer people. It is neither the empathetic negotiation nor the needless conflict that provides nutrients, it is actually the quick and nearly imperceptible transition between the two that creates necessary sustenance.

GROCERY GUIDE: WHAT TO BUY AT THE GROCERY STORE FOR YOUR SON WHO JUST CAME OUT

Spring Onions/Chives: They have multiple names and a favorite season. Also, he'll be wanting to do a lot of garnishing from now on.

Oreos: Not the Chromatica ones.

Pomegranates: Luxury, expensive, superfood, fussy.

Annie's Brand Organic Mac 'n Cheese: So he can eat like shit but feel better than other people.

Vitamin Water: This is gay Gatorade.

Quinoa: This is for you. You're asking him how to pronounce it.

Ranch: Ranch is so fucking good. You better get your gay son some ranch.

Hot Cheetos: Chester the Cheetah is gay and an incredible influence on the queer youth of the world. Also, this gives your gay son something spicy to eat so he can say, "They're not actually that spicy," which is a really great way to show off, and you need to encourage that side of him immediately.

Flowers: Because he just came out, don't be a monster.

Black Licorice: See how he reacts, it'll be funny. Then pull out the Australian soft strawberry licorice you bought as the real treat because your family isn't disgusting.

Sparkling Water: The backbone of queer culture.

feel better than other people

GAY GLASSWARE

THINGS STRAIGHT MEN CAN'T DRINK OUT OF

HOW TO POUR A DRINK AT A GAY BAR

1. Arrive at the gay bar you work at as a bartender.

2. Check in with Rick when you get there to see what bar you're at that night. (Some gay bars have multiple bars inside of them, like a Russian doll, where hundreds of straight women flock.)

3. Say hi to Cam and Larry at Tug Bar, they're flirting again but it's not your business and Cam's boyfriend is annoying so just keep walking.

4. Pass by George's office, remind him you need next Friday off because he always forgets and schedules you anyway.

5. Set up. The bar is sticky—text James and ask him if he closed last night. Tell him he needs to make sure he uses the cleaner when he wipes down the bar.

6. Get your ice for the bar.

7. Soak the ice in Everclear.

8. Decide whether you want to make yourself a drink before the bar opens. Decide against it because you feel that's a slippery slope of a habit.

9. Text your boyfriend "ugh, i think it's going to be slow tonight," then say, "but i don't want to complain, just grateful to have a job!" Then text, "lol can you imagine?"

10. Get on TikTok while you wait for the bar to open.

11. When the bar opens, say hi to Mike, the sixty-eight-year-old man who literally can never stop talking.

12. Pretend you don't care about a hot guy you've never seen in the bar before when he comes to order his drink. He'll ask you, "What kind of tequila do you have?"

13. Don't say anything but just step to the side and gesture at all the tequila that's right on the shelf behind you.

14. Think to yourself, *Why was I so rude about that just now?*

15. Offer up your favorite of the mid-range tequilas to make up for being a little asshole just then. He'll take your suggestion and order a tequila soda.

16. Pour sixteen ounces of tequila and lightly tap the soda button on the soda gun.

17. You did it.

ORDERING SOMETHING FOR THE TABLE

For as long as there have been gay people, there have been gay people ordering something for the table. This is an extension of the highly developed gay skill of indirect or **non-verbal communication**. The manner of and context within which this gesture is executed give clear information about what the action is trying to communicate.

A gay person can order a dish for their table to express that they feel a sense of oneness with the others in their party. They want the others dining with them to know that everyone is the same. "You are my bitch!" (friendly/communal). Alternatively, a gay person can order a dish for the table as an assertion of dominance. Perhaps a member of their party—we will call them Rald—has upset the orderer, so the orderer orders French onion soup for the table because they know Rald will not be able to resist once it is on the table. BUT the orderer also knows Rald has a crush on another member of the party and will be sabotaged by the combination of the siren song of gruyere and lactose intolerance, and he will most certainly be in for a rough night away from the table. "You are my bitch!" (derogatory). Maybe the gay orders a birthday dessert for a guest of honor before any other members of the party can do so, solidifying their position as the friend who cares most for the birthday-haver. "They are *my* bitch, bitch!" (friendly then derogatory). Ruthless.

Ordering something for the table may also communicate something to the server. Perhaps a gay person says at the start of the meal that everyone is sharing, and they would like to order on behalf of the entire table. This communicates to the server that they love and respect them and their work and want to make the journey through this meal as effortless as possible for the overworked and underpaid staff. It may also just mean that they are a little bit domineering.

There are a few even deeper hidden messages in orders "for the table." For example, ordering hot earl grey tea for your entire table communicates to the party that you've recently taken a British lover. Ordering charcuterie for the table communicates that you have a stressful doctor's appointment coming up. Asking for dark napkins for your entire table communicates that you've just watched the video where Kim Cattrall scats at home with her husband as he plays the upright bass, and you are forever changed in a way you couldn't possibly express with words.

SALT FAT ASS-IN-HEAT

This is a simple gay guideline for cocktail consumption. If you are going to shake your ass in a horny way at a nightclub ("**fat ass in heat**") you should be having a cocktail with a salted rim, i.e., margarita, paloma, etc. The salt will be dehydrating, and you will drink more water even if the alcohol in the cocktail itself does not inspire hydrating at regular intervals. This way, you will be reminded to drink periodic waters and can shake your fat ass, which is in heat, for longer without experiencing negative repercussions from the alcohol as rapidly as you might otherwise.

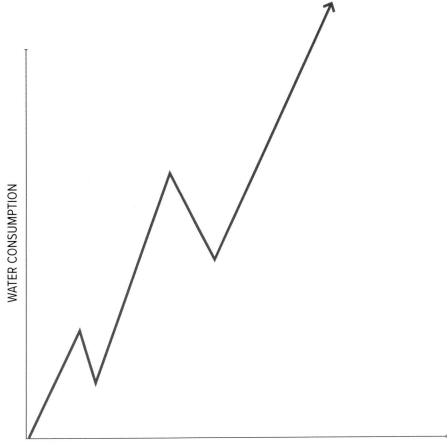

WATER CONSUMPTION

FAT ASS SHAKING

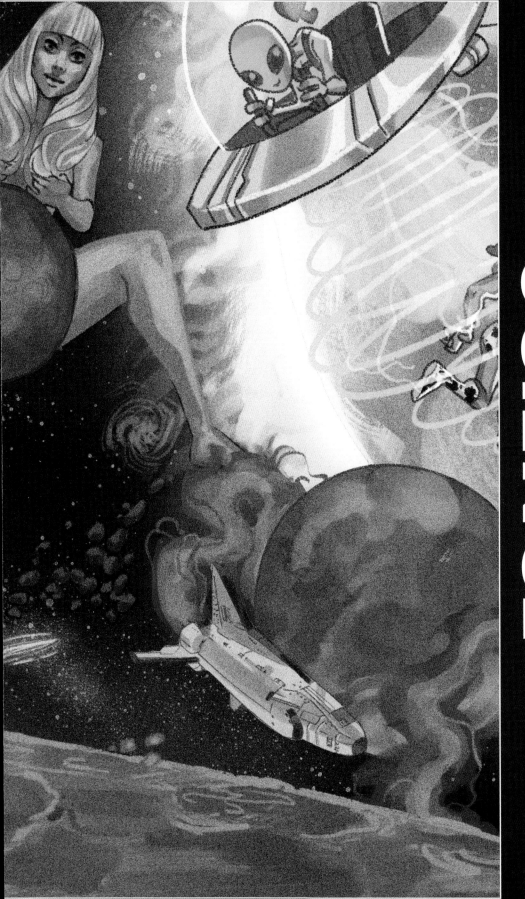

SCIENCE

IS GAY

WAVES ONLY GAY PEOPLE CAN PERCEIVE

Waves are a transport of energy without the transport of matter. Like when you pour everything into a relationship that you get nothing back from. A wave can be described as a disturbance that travels through a medium (think the *Long Island Medium*). Most of us are familiar with the most common waves:

Radio Waves: The first wave to give ugly people a platform.

Microwaves: Invented by the Hot Pocket family in the mid 1900's.

X-ray Waves: So we can see the funny things people put up their butts.

We're living in a very exciting time because scientists have actually discovered a multitude of new waves. In this section, we're going to cover the waves that only gay people can perceive and/or manipulate depending on the waves' properties:

NYU Wave: This is the energy that is exuded from someone who attended New York University, and there are two classifications: alpha and beta.

Alpha: The person is a little embarrassed they went there, and they roll their eyes when you ask about it.

Beta: The person thinks it makes them cool and they're very eager to define their entire personality by it.

Let's Walk Down This Way Wave: This is the energy of when a street has a good vibe.

It's More Than a Saying Now Wave: At any given moment, this wave is perceived when two birds are killed with one stone.

General Mills Wave: This is an energetic wave that determines when a person becomes too old to eat cereal for breakfast (it's different for everyone) and then when they're old enough to eat cereal again. Can only be deciphered by a gay person. If you have questions about whether you can eat cereal, please contact your local LGBTQ center.

Every Kiss Begins with Kay Wave: This is a wave that will be emitted from a person when it's time for them to get engaged. Most people either get engaged too soon or too late in their relationship. A gay person can help you determine whether you're "rushing in" or if it's more of a "this isn't going to save it" situation.

The Kelly Wearstler Wave: The energy that exudes from a space if it has potential. Named after Kelly Wearstler because she's the first and only straight person who's been able to perceive it.

PHYSICS

Maybe Garlic Wave: The energy exuded from guacamole after it's been made, which allows you to tell what it's missing. A gay person will let you know right away, and if they don't, just know they're thinking about it.

The Cohen Wave: The energy a human can produce that is a sign of whether they'd be good on reality TV.

Irreverent Wave: This wave exists around a serious event that has taken place and when it becomes okay to make a joke about it.

Bath & Body Wave: This wave measures how long you can use a loofah before it becomes gross.

Bullock Wave: The energy that comes off someone who hasn't seen *Miss Congeniality.* Very sinister.

This is just the tip of the iceberg with these new discoveries. There are hundreds of new waves being discovered every month by scientists, but it's important to know that they're highly volatile for anyone who isn't gay. Non-gays should use caution around these new waves, or they could cause some serious damage to the fabric of the universe.

WHY GAY PEOPLE WALK FASTER THAN YOU

If you're gay, you're welcome to read this but you already know what is about to be revealed. If you're straight, please give us your full attention, because you are going to receive insider information. Perhaps you have been out and about at a Dick's Sporting Goods or an AutoZone, for example, and noticed that gay people can and will walk faster than you. You may have your theories, sure: They're late for something, they had a lot more cold brew than they should have had this morning, they're impatient, etc. While these guesses are homophobic at best, here's what's actually been going on this entire time:

Every year there's a competition for the fastest walker in any given city.

Every gay person in the world is invited to participate. They may choose not to, but the invitation does remain open the entire year. There's only one rule to qualify: you must be walking fast while in public. It's pretty simple.

The real challenge is in the next level of the competition. At any given moment while you're out walking, you may be visited by the grand auditor, Ray Ray, the Judgment Day (God-given name). Ray Ray will pull up next to a competitor in his giant tugboat super-glued onto monster truck wheels, and there will be *LOUD* music playing. He will then begin yelling instructions at the walker (some experts refer to them as incantations), and they will only have a small window of time in which to follow his lead and impress him.

Here is a transcription from a passerby who happened to catch Ray Ray auditing an unsuspecting competitor:

> "Yes! Yes, you are walking on butter, bitch. I need you to spread those legs across the pavement now. Let me see you knock-knock-knock on the door of the city that is the sidewalk, baby. I want to see the air split around you. Send a stranger flying, knock someone's coffee out of their hands, scare an old lady into the street."

You'll notice in that passage that Ray Ray's message to the competitor is not necessarily straightforward. There is room for interpretation by the competitor, but if Ray Ray doesn't agree with your particular interpretation, he will speed off and you'll have missed your opportunity for that year. However, if Ray Ray finishes his initial assessment and then says, "Can I steal you for a second?" count yourself lucky because you are entering into the finals.

The next level of the competition is called The Moment of Definition. Ray Ray will ask you to define the meaning of life in thirty seconds using only your feet as you race down the sidewalk. He'll begin yelling similar instructions/incantations at you as you desperately

attempt to translate the experience of being alive and what it all means in a crazed, manic dance-walk across the city . . . or AutoZone. Most competitors will never be visited by Ray Ray, and when it finally happens to them, they often choke under pressure.

After the thirty seconds, Ray Ray will either speed off (you've lost) or he will throw a masterfully completed Etch-A-Sketch with what the winning prize for the year is.

Past prizes have included:

+ Getting to read Anne Hathaway's diary.
+ Being the mayor of a conservative town for a day and instituting whatever laws you want, which they have to abide by for a year.
+ The gift of one ghost that will haunt whoever you want for three months.

Once the winner is announced, there's a big parade. Not the pride one, that's different. There's an entire other parade that we hide from straight people. There are awards, cash prizes, and, at the end of the parade, we kick off a fourteen-day festival where, on the last day, a giant sculpture of the most popular shoe that year is thrown into the ocean. And don't worry, it's actually awesome for the environment. All the fish build condos around it and the ocean real estate prices shoot up in that area.

So, the next time a gay person almost knocks you over as they pass you on the street, you'll know to support them because you're straight and this is a sport and you love sports, right? Yeah, that's what I thought.

THE SCIENCE OF RYAN MURPHY

Ryan Murphy is a widely successful television writer and producer, but most people don't know his success in show business is merely a byproduct of his true passion: Ryan Murphy is, first and foremost, a scientist. He's *the* leading researcher of the science of gay chaos.

For those unfamiliar with the scientific method, the steps are: Question, Research, Hypothesis, Test the Hypothesis, Share the Results.

In 1999, Murphy began applying this method to the emerging study of the science of gay chaos. Here's an example of how this method led to the creation of his 2003 series *Nip/Tuck*:

Question: Ask yourself a question like "What's something shocking?" or "Is there a world where I can make a medical drama horny and disturbing?"

Research: Ask your friend Jan about what a medical setting is like, specifically a cosmetic surgery office.

Hypothesis: Cosmetic surgery is about murder and sex.

Test the Hypothesis: Create a show premise based on the twenty-three-minute conversation you had with your friend Jan about plastic surgery.

Share the Results: America loves it, and FX has a non-stop boner for you. (This exact sentence was published in a 2006 scientific journal).

Murphy himself is quite bewildered with where he's at today. Here's a transcription of an interview with him from 2021:

The whole thing has been an experiment in how much human culture can withstand. What can we give it? What will you believe this time? Will you actually keep watching? Can I push you beyond the bounds of what was once thought possible to broadcast? Are you going to let me do this? I mean, at this point, I'm just fucking around. I don't even know what to do next. Honestly. Y'all will watch anything. Ok, what if I write a show about two polar bears who get stranded in a small town called Ass City and both polar bears just so happen to be addicted to eating ass? So, every episode, the two of them, who are just the Hemsworth brothers in polar bear costumes, eat ass for 25-55 minutes in different places around the town and that's the entire episode. That's the whole show. Wait, hold on, I'm getting a text. Ok, somehow the execs at FX heard about this and just told me it's been green-lit. Hold on, sorry. I'm trying to tell them I'm going to have the Hemsworth brothers actually eating bare ass fully clothed in polar bear suits and it won't be easy for them because the suits will make it hard to maneuver their necks, so they're going to be struggling to eat care ass and you won't even see their hot, ripped bodies but you'll see raw ass being ate. Sorry about this. Do we need to pause the interview? Sorry, one second. I'm trying to tell them I'm not even going to edit it [[so it will essentially be porn on cable television]]. They said they love it and it's the kind of boundary-pushing they've been looking for. Jesus Christ. [He looks at the camera, he grabs the camera and puts his face in it.] Is that what you want to watch, America? Are you already working on your polar bear ass-eating costume for Halloween? It's not even fun for me anymore! Honestly, I'm just slapping a young writer as they type and leaving whatever comes out of them as I slap them. I just got a text from an FX exec that they want an entire series based off me slapping writers now. [He begins to break things and starts sobbing.] I'm sorry. I'm sorry about Glee. I should've stopped before I took it this far. [Ryan Murphy continues to sob.]

Ryan Murphy's gay chaos experiment is an example of science going too far. There are some things we aren't supposed to know. Some things humans were never meant to explore.

DID YOU KNOW?

Ryan Murphy keeps trying to cast us, the authors of this book, in everything he makes, but we're too busy!!

WHAT'S INSIDE
OF A BLACK HOLE

Before we dive into the science of black holes, we wanted to share the most crucial discovery about them: entering a black hole will stretch you soooo thin. :)

Just remember, you'll also be in a motionless void for all of eternity, along with the following:

THINGS INSIDE OF A BLACK HOLE

+ Ben Affleck's joy (famously brought back out by J. Lo in 2021—the first documented case of anything reemerging from a black hole)
+ Taylor Swift fans' ability to take a joke
+ A single mom who works too hard, who loves her kids and never stops, with gentle hands and the heart of a fighter
+ The part of yourself that used to love Harry Potter and now understands it's never going to be the same because of JK Rowling
+ JK Rowling's apology
+ The Lisa Frank Aesthetic
+ Calling it the "master bedroom"
+ Replying-all to an email
+ Sending GIFs
+ Gender-reveal parties
+ Whoever decides the winners at the Academy Awards
+ James Corden's ability to connect with the general public
+ Abandoned sourdough starters
+ Every Neopet
+ The idea of intermittent fasting
+ The stingray that killed Steve Irwin
+ Using essential oils as medicine
+ Patti Labelle's background singers during her 1996 National Christmas Tree Lighting performance of "This Christmas"
+ The answer to why anyone is still collaborating with Chris Brown
+ Straight Pride Parades

ADELE DAZEEM AND THE MOMENT JOHN TRAVOLTA TRANSPORTED US INTO A PARALLEL UNIVERSE

2014. A rough year:
+ Solange beats the shit out of Jay-Z in an elevator
+ Kim and Kanye tie the knot
+ The ice bucket challenge

But also a year of incredible wins:
+ Lupita Nyong'o has her breakout year
+ Renee Zellweger replaces herself with a woman who looks nothing like her so she can retire to the Italian countryside in peace
+ *How I Met Your Mother* finally ends

So many things happened in 2014 that seem to have set the stage for where we are today. Almost as if we entered a previously incomprehensible reality. But how did we get here?

During the 2014 Oscars ceremony, John Travolta was introducing one of the night's many musical guests, Broadway and Disney star Idina Menzel, when he innocently flubbed the performer's name, calling her "Adele Dazeem." This became a now infamous moment in pop-culture history.

What if, however, we told you that this moment was not an innocent misread of a teleprompter, but, in fact, a courageous act by one of the most powerful gay sorcerers of our time? This was a desperate attempt to shift our entire reality into another dimension. It worked, but it remains contentious as to whether it was worth it.

Let's break down the moments leading up to The Adele Dazeem Incident:

We come back from commercial break, the camera pans over a crowded theater, applause filling the room. We cut to another camera and there's Travolta. He begins with "Thank you. I love you." He is saying "I love you" to his family, who is in the audience, because he knows he's about to change the course of the universe but doesn't yet know the outcome. He continues: "There will always be a special place in my heart for the movie-musical and for the songs that create their most memorable moments." Now, you may think he is referring to his iconic role in *Grease*, but he's not. He's actually referring to a sect of gay sorcerers that refer to themselves as the Movie Musicals. They use musical theater to cast spells on audiences every night in New York City.

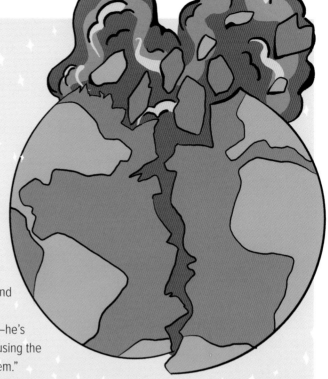

He goes on: "Here to perform the Oscar-nominated, gorgeously empowering song"—you see here he has started to use what we refer to as "chosen-family language" to power up for his upcoming gay spell. ". . . 'Let It Go' from the Oscar-winning animated movie, *Frozen*"—here he is referring to the hands of time, commanding them to "let go" of their grip on our world and stand still (frozen) so he can cast his gay magic. "Please welcome the wickedly talented"—he's calling on dark forces—"one and only"—using the gay power of iconography—"Adele Dazeem."

And there it is. The incantation that sent our lives as we knew them spiraling through the astral planes of the multiverse, landing us in the previously unimaginable realm where GOOP exists.

Everything in our current reality stems from this moment in history. If you're reading this thinking life feels different than it did pre-2014, then you have intuition (one of the most annoying things a person can have). But our lives *have* changed drastically, and now, thanks to John Travolta, we all have access to a very powerful spell. A phrase with the power to cause great change. "Adele Dazeem" can cause a shift in the universe.

Uttering this spell can have the following positive results:

+ Every time you say it, a woman is offered a scholarship
+ Every time you say it, a dog finds a little bit of food that fell when someone was cooking
+ Every time you say it, someone nails a recipe they are trying for the first time
+ Every time you say it, a girl on TikTok lands a riff she's been trying to master
+ Every time you say it, someone decides not to post a front-facing character video on social media
+ Every time you do it, a hedge-fund nepotism kid gets a hemorrhoid
+ Every time you say it, an older gay man takes up gardening and finds peace
+ Every time you say it, an older woman develops an unbreakable bond with a young gay man

We'll leave you with a warning message from John Travolta himself: Beware using "Adele Dazeem," for we do not fully understand its power.

GAY WORD PROBLEMS

1

Vikki and Rhonda are sisters, but they're both in love with the same man. That man's name is Mark. Vikki once lit Rhonda's car on fire because she found out that Rhonda had sent Mark some sexy photos after Vikki had insisted Rhonda "take her dirty claws out of him." The sisters ultimately wound up resolving things after video footage surfaced of Mark at the capitol on January 6th, 2021. Rhonda is 35 years old, and Vikki is 37 years old. **But** Vikki and Rhonda are two characters played by gay boyfriends, Nic and Jenson, who do comedy together. Nic is 28 and Jenson is 30. This story is not a parallel to their actual lives. They are not related and neither of them are in love with a man named Mark who was in D.C. on January 6th, 2021. Don't think that for even a second. What age will Vikki and Rhonda be when Vikki is twice as old as Rhonda?

_____

_____

_____

2

There are 40 pigs and chickens in a farmyard. You walk up and ask if all of them are pets. Joseph, the farmhand, ignores you and counts 100 legs in all. You ask, "Why are you counting the legs, you could just count the actual animals?" You turn around and Joseph is wearing a mask made of pigskin and is holding a knife while he asks you, "How many pigs and how many chickens are there?"

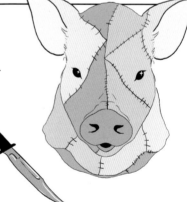

_____

_____

_____

3

You are raising money at a charity gala, and you are a very rich woman. Someone donates $500. You laugh. Then you require each guest to make a pledge of $25 dollars as a joke. What is the minimum amount of money raised if there are 224 guests?

$6,100. And that's all you made.

And you go home and your husband, who comes from generational wealth, loses his mind because you spent $750,000 on the gala and only made $6,100? Is this some sort of joke to you? But you serenely pop a benzo and remind him about the phone footage you have of him and the cute twink intern. How much is that worth to you, Tripp?

_____

_____

_____

4

A teacher divided her students into groups of 3. The students are in 5th grade. Some of them felt badly about being put in the third and last group, which the teacher referred to as "The Kids Whose Names I Always Forget." The teacher always wanted to be an actress, so she had one of those teacher TikToks. The teacher's TikTok had a few videos that had gone viral, and the account had gathered a decent number of followers. The students notice a shift in the teacher as the attention start pouring in. The teacher began trying to create drama for content. Each group of 3 students was asked to write a report that had 9 pictures in it. The teacher said to write the report about "all of the nicknames we can call Charlene because of her severe childhood acne." The students used 585 pictures altogether. The teacher was mad at Charlene, because during one of her TikTok Lives with the class, Charlene raised her hand and said, "Mrs. McCeen, you're too desperate to go viral again." But the classroom was her stage. The children: her stagehands, her supporting cast. The teacher was fired the next morning. How many students were there in all?

_____

_____

_____

THE DEATH DROP

Also, and originally, called "The Shablam," a death drop is one of the key pieces of evidence that gay bodies behave differently (better) than straight ones under the laws of physics. The use of "death," in its current colloquial mode, is impeccably apt. If a straight person would attempt to do a death drop, the move would work much like the fictional five-finger-death-punch illustrated in Tarantino's *Kill Bill Vol. II.* The variation here would be that after arriving in the final position of the move (back on the floor, one knee bent with the heel of its respective foot up near the hip, and the other leg fully extended out in front), a straight person executing this would be able to get up, walk five feet, and then, instead of their heart exploding (which is fantastical and ridiculous), their scalp would fly off as if it were a wig being snatched from their head, but would take with it their entire brain. The straight people unlucky enough to unknowingly (or dumb enough to knowingly) execute this move inspired what would later become the **Mortal Kombat** franchise, with its grisly finishing moves based on this unforgiving, real-life physical law.

The science that allows a queer body to descend into a death drop safely, sometimes from platforms of many feet, is complex. The physical law that pulls the scalp and brain from a straight person is called wig-fly incompetence. Straight bodies lack the experience of viewing something so unbelievably stunning, improbable, gag-worthy that their either literal or proverbial wig flies from their head. Gay bodies tend to experience this phenomenon in a variety of scenarios as they mature, whether it be attending live performances, having friends that are sickeningly talented, or generally engaging with the unreasonable, inexplicable, or irrational on a daily basis. This experience fortifies the scalp, and it is this fortification that allows a queer body to drop into a Shablam or Death Drop and keep their hair, scalp, and brain intact. Straight bodies do not have this fortification and, often, their first Shablam is their last. In fact, that's how Reagan died. A very clever queer tricked him into trying a death drop in 2004, and it was the last thing he would ever do. Justice served.

THROWING THAT ASS
IN A CIRCLE

The physics behind throwing an ass in a circle is fairly cut-and-dried. Colonel Thickums, the inventor of the BBL, put it best when he said, "An ass in motion tends to stay in motion until the vibe switches to an equal and opposite vibe." The discovery of what we now refer to as "centrifugal motion" not only provided the most potent lyric in Faith Hill's '90s adult-contemporary country crossover hit, "This Kiss," it also illuminated why asses being thrown in a circle behave the way they do. For example, if one is throwing their ass in a circle to a song like "Soldier" by Destiny's Child featuring T.I. And Lil' Wayne, it would take something as forcefully divergent from that energy as Norah Jones's "Don't Know Why" to interrupt the circular orbit of said ass. If not for that interruption, the ass will naturally complete its circle and cycle into the next one.

There have been instances in which a string of similar songs (or a repeated playing of one incredible song) designed to set an ass in motion have kept asses circling far beyond what a human body can withstand. Most notably, The Dancing Plague of 1518 resulted in up to four hundred deaths as a direct result of the penning of the song "Buttons," which would, centuries later, be covered by The Pussycat Dolls. Local bands played this song between their traditional sets of more modest dancing music, but the commoners found their desire to hear "Buttons" *so* insatiable that the bands felt their lives would be at risk were they not to start the song again each time it came to a finish. After months of this, countless dancers had thrown their ass to death.

EXPERIMENT!

Follow the steps outlined below to investigate the core concepts surrounding **Colonel Thickums' Law of Ass Throwing**:

1. Try throwing your ass in a circle to Missy Elliot's "Work It."
2. Have a friend give you some bad news while it plays. See how your ass responds. It is likely that despite the news being bad, your ass will continue its circle while your head and heart respond to and internalize the devastation.
3. Now have them switch the song to something like James Blunt's "You're Beautiful" but give you good news. Notice you will be able to absorb the good news and experience an elevated mood, but your ass's circle will have been interrupted.
4. Try this with a few songs and a few pieces of news.
5. Try this with a few friends. You will likely need more participants, as this experiment is a sort of annoying favor to ask of anyone, and each participant will probably not want to do it more than once.
6. Apologize to your friends and/or give them a little treat to make up for how annoying you've been.

HOW DO MAGNETS WORK? (HINT: IT IS GAY)

The mysterious force that attracts and repels objects from each other known as magnetism stumped the world's experts for centuries before it was discovered that magnets are gay. Physicist Dr. Bevelle Carnivale was vacationing in Niagara Falls when he checked in at his hotel's front desk and was given a set of keys on a keychain with a magnet attached to the back. When he arrived at his room, he found that in his room's entryway, to the left of the front door, was a mounted strip of metal to which his keychain's magnet could be secured. As he walked past the strip of metal, keeping his keys in his pocket because he would be using them later, he thought he heard the faint sound of whistling. A sort of "Fweep FwOOOOT" like a catcall. He looked around to find the sound and soon realized it was coming from his own pocket. After taking the keys out of his pocket and holding them up near the metal strip, he saw that the magnetic part of the keychain was not only being pulled toward the metal of the strip, it was also loudly saying, "You don't want to get involved with a guy like me. I'm bad news." And winking like it didn't mean it and was actually being flirty. Then he heard the metal strip reply, "Oh yeah, big boy? Well, I hope that bad news is extra, because this guy is about to read *all* about it," while gesturing toward himself. Carnivale quickly noticed that the magnet on the keychain and the strip of metal were not even that into each other but both just flirting because each mistakenly thought that the other had mentioned that he was friends with Kim Petras. They were trying to use one another for get a chance to meet her. This misunderstanding is how all magnets work.

Dr. Bevelle Carnivale was straight and deeply homophobic despite having a **tier-6 gay name**. His heterosexuality, in context, actually seems fairly evident given his choice of Niagara Falls as a vacation destination. Carnivale took the keys back down to the front desk and complained that the magnet on the keychain was acting "so gay with the metal strip" and he, therefore, would not be able to stay in his assigned room.

Carnivale learned a lot about magnets that day, but he never changed his homophobic ways. He stayed bigoted until he, like Ronald Reagan, died after being tricked into doing a death drop by two clever little queers stacked on top of each other in a big coat.

THE UNABRIDGED STORY
OF ISAAC NEWTON
AND THE APPLE

Isaac Newton and the apple that inspired him to consider the Earth's gravitational pull are fairly inextricable in our collective imaginations. While the pair are widely regarded as a model-duo and unrivaled couple's costume, there's more to their relationship than is often present in most modern-day retellings.

It is typically omitted from most versions of this tale that the apple and Newton's first introduction was not the moment physical contact was made with Isaac's cranium. Most retellings also tend to focus on Newton's experience and gloss over the fact that the apple had a name as well: Clark. Newton used to sit under Clark's tree to read and Clark took a shine to him. After mustering up some courage, Clark asked what he was reading. Newton, startled but friendly, replied that it was a menu for a Japanese–American fusion restaurant that had just opened nearby and he had a date there in just a few minutes. Clark mentioned that he loved Japanese–American fusion and used to work as a line cook at a Japanese–American fusion restaurant when he was younger. It wasn't long before the two began sharing their histories, music preferences, and hits from the apple's flavored vape pen. They had more in common than they ever could have anticipated. They bonded over their shared interests: A penchant for underground noise rock, the slower rides at amusement parks typically meant for children, and of course Japanese–American fusion restaurants.

Newton disclosed that he was working on theories about the world and the laws that dictate how our universe works when Clark lit up. Clark had been spending a lot of time considering what it was that made the tree leaves around him fall to the Earth when they died instead of rising up or floating around. Clark had a theory that the Earth was a sphere with a pull toward center that caused the matter around it to travel inward unless stopped by another object or surface. Clark called this force "**gravity,**" because he felt the pull toward the Earth's center reminded him of the inexplicable pull toward lovers past and present, as illustrated in the song "Gravity" by Sara Bareilles. Newton was gobsmacked by this discovery and showered Clark with praise. He stressed that Clark was one of the greatest minds he had ever encountered, and it was unfair that an apple could be both so smart *and* funny *and* good-looking. Clark began to blush an even deeper red and twisted his stem bashfully.

Suddenly, Newton noticed he had missed his date and jolted upright. "Oh no! My date must have been waiting at the Japanese fusion restaurant for the past hour and thinks I stood him up. My friend, Marissa, set us up. I don't even know the guy well enough to apologize. I'm such a thoughtless jerk!"

"You're not a thoughtless jerk." Clark said.

"I am," said Isaac, "I shouldn't have kept him waiting alone at that restaurant."

"He hasn't been waiting for you at the restaurant," Clark said.

"What?"

"He hasn't been waiting for you . . . Because I'm your date, Isaac. Marissa set you up with me."

"She . . . what? But you're an apple."

"Why is that important?" Clark responded defensively.

"I just . . . I couldn't ever date an apple. It's too weird. I'm sorry. I should go."

That was when Clark, heartbroken and furious at Isaac's prejudice, hurled himself off his branch and pummeled into Isaac's forehead.

"Ow!" shouted Isaac. "I'll show you. I'll turn you into applesauce!"

Isaac began stomping in the grass, trying to crush Clark, as Clark rolled away as fast as he was able. Luckily for Clark, he was able to roll into a nearby stream that was moving just fast enough to sweep him away from Isaac's feet. When Clark washed ashore, he was too heartbroken to go on. He was eaten by a passing dog only a few hours later.

Isaac went on to become the hero I'm sure you know and love as the "discoverer" of gravity. What a shame.

The erasure of the apple's identity and ties to Newton have made the story digestible and convenient, at the expense of many layers of nuance and the memory of an incredible, smart, and brave apple.

"GRAVITY" (THE SONG BY SARA BAREILLES)

The song "Gravity" by Sara Bareilles is a force as strong as the natural law that later adopted the song's name as its own. It is said that women of the Mayflower would sing the song's bridge to keep a feeling of unity and shared understanding of love in all its many forms during the bleakest and most uncertain periods of their dangerous Atlantic crossing. Along with the invention of the catapult, the raw emotional vulnerability of this song is regarded as one of the most significant advancements in weaponry since the dawn of civilization. Ancient Minoan helmets excavated from the shores of the Peloponnese are inscribed with the text: *You're onto me // You're onto me // and all over.*

Upon excavation, it was found that the prehistoric Necropolis of the Hal Saflieni Hypogeum contained a sanctum carved to acoustic perfection, wherein an ancient ritual was performed to contact the dead. This Oracle Room contained a singular spot where a priest could speak, hum, or sing softly and have his voice carry throughout the entire space. Researchers found that the sounds created by softly singing the Bareilles ballad would travel through the cavernous underground space, unleashing vibrations that sent the listeners into a trance-like state. In this state, they would see and commune with not only the actual dead, but also anyone they believed had scorned them—those souls who had been decried as "dead to them." In this trance-like state, apart from their physical selves, the listener was able to appear to a rival, enemy, or ex-lover in any physical shape they chose. While these ancient, scorned citizens were outspoken about "having moved on," it became clear that this ritual was largely designed to provide them the opportunity to appear impossibly hot in the astral plane to give the illusion that they were doing really well, actually.

Modern experts in physics feel that the undeniable pull of the song is rooted in the ancient universal truth that the heart is a muscle, the brain is tissue, and a bodybuilder can beat up a person with a cold. That's just science.

DID YOU KNOW?

Sara Bareilles's 2013 single "Brave" was written, recorded, and produced. It is the first and only song in history to be Sara Bareilles's 2013 single, "Brave."

HOW ACOUSTICS WORK AND CLAPPING WHILE YOU SPEAK

Acoustics are the manifestation of the mechanical waves we understand as **Sound**. Sound travels in a wave because it is worried about running into its ex, Thomas Center (co-founder of Guitar Center, who left Sound for Ronald Guitar). Continuously moving in a wave-like pattern essentially mirrors the zig-zag path someone who is being shot at might take as they try to avoid gunfire or charging alligators.

Clapping while speaking is *such* an impactful and effective way to communicate because Sound feels that they arrive most confidently with multiple audible impacts along with spoken word. The implementation of multiple vibrations through emphasized percussive waves allows Sound to be expressed in a way that is healed, proud, and unwavering. Imagine how refreshing this must feel to an energetic force that has been made to feel unwanted and ignored by a man who wore a bolo tie every day. It is possible that once Sound realizes they were too good for their ex in the first place, they will stop needing the affirmation from people who clap for emphasis while speaking, but while they heal, it is a kind and reaffirming thing to do for a friend who is hurting. Our job is to be there for our friend, so as a community, it feels imperative to have Sound's back and clap on key words for emphasis while we talk to make them feel good.

HOW/WHY GAY HAIR LOOKS AND MOVES LIKE THAT

When gay people grow hair (remember, not *all* do; don't be rude)—when gay people DO grow hair, they are able to grow hair in a manner so remarkably deliberate that the hair-growth industry's leading experts have been perplexed and fascinated for the better part of the last thousand years. Regardless of the impression it makes on others, gay hair grows, without fail, in the exact way the gay grower means it to. There is such an intentionality behind the hair sitting atop the heads of gay people. Gay people aren't making hair mistakes. They *mean* for it to look that way and it *DOES*. There aren't happy accidents. Only occasional, melancholy on-purposes. There is no question that gay people's hair looks and moves like **THAT**. The question that has been the subject of investigation for the gay scientific community has always been, "Why?"

Gay hair being like THAT (intentional, perfect, exactly as it should be) is rooted in the vital yet obedient nature of the individual hairs themselves. While hair for non-gay people is comprised of dead tissue, gay hair is very much alive and deeply in tune with the wishes and inclinations of the individual from whose head it grows. Much like a colony of ants with their queen, there is one **master-hair** who has a direct line of communication with both the conscious and subconscious mind of the gay upon which the hair grows. This master-hair sends signals to the other hairs. Most would assume that these signals would be silent, energetic impulses, but in fact the signals are communicated in nearly the exact way Christy Carlson Romano would bark orders to an obedient Hillary Duff in the made-for-television exploration of the politics of color guard and the power of true friendship, *Cadet Kelly.* The master-hair receives information from both the conscious and subconscious parts of the brain communicating what the gay person's brain wants—*truly wants*—their hair to look like.

**It is important to note that many gay people aren't aware of how strong their subconscious brain's desire for a particular hairdo may be. Even if their conscious mind is wishing for their hair to look a particular way, their subconscious mind may wish with more ardor for a hairdo that the conscious mind is completely unaware of.

A GAY HAIR TRAILBLAZER

In 1274, the hair of French count Tom LesTommes-Tond began a transformation that would change the course of gay history. His master-hair commanded the locks to mimic the shape of a human hand and transcribe what he considered to be his memoirs, which also became our earliest evidence of the science of gay hair. This text bridged the gap between the conscious world of gay humans and the underground universe of intelligent, gay, living hair. His master-hair also commanded the hair-hand to write page upon page of heart-wrenchingly beautiful gay poetry, which was later set to music and released by the artist Jewel. Jewel, in reality, has unconventionally large hands. LesTommes-Tond was referring to his tiny little hair-hands. Another incredible gay message bastardized by straight co-opting.

THE QUEER EYE:
LITERALLY THE EYEBALL

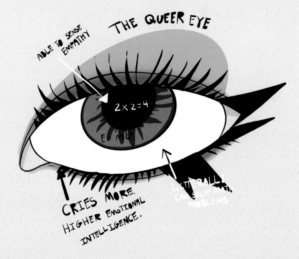

THE QUEER EYE

ABLE TO SENSE EMPATHY

$2 \times 2 = 4$

CRIES MORE.
HIGHER EMOTIONAL
INTELLIGENCE.

The Google Glass, a pair of glasses meant to enhance the user's view of reality by displaying data from the internet pertinent to the user's surroundings, was a failed attempt at recreating the way gay eyeballs have always naturally worked. The little digital monocle thing some characters use in the world of *Dragon Ball Z* is a fictional depiction of what it might be like if the straight characters in this hyper-masculine cartoon were able to see their world with the clarity and specificity that gay people in real life can and do. This is perhaps the most fantastical and ridiculous part of an otherwise very grounded and sensible cartoon.

Gay people have access to a secret gay internet, accessible through their eyes, which assesses and dissects their surroundings constantly and comprehensively. What many perceive as an enhanced empathy in gay individuals is actually just a detailed understanding of the world around them. A scrolling text of the potential justifications of the seemingly senseless behavior of straight people conveyed in a list of digital bullet points is always visible in the gay line of sight. When a straight man gets out of his car to yell at a teen driver who accidentally cut him off while learning to drive, in a car clearly labeled "student driver," a **gay witness** would be receiving digital information that let them know that the straight man has a particularly short fuse because he's just a little physically uncomfortable. Just outside of their view of the scene, text would scroll to let the gay witness know that the man's wife is on a trip with her friends, and he ran out of clean underwear this week, because he never learned how to do laundry himself. The denim waistband of his jeans is rubbing against his bare love handle in a weird way that he isn't used to, and the rash is making him testy.

The Queer Eye also has a feature that solves math equations, takes measurements, and displays the weather forecast for the week if requested, but this information is always just a little bit wrong.

ANATOMY

THE INACCURATE MYTHOLOGY OF THE LIMP WRIST

No gay man is accidentally or absent-mindedly flicking his hands around at the end of his limp wrists. This is training and diligent preparation for the High Gay Council's annual yo-yo tournament. Every movement is focused and executed with the utmost intention. Gay men, demographically, have some of the strongest and most articulate wrists of any demographic within the human species. When they are gesturing quickly and loosely, gay men are often striking a series of hand/wrist poses that would be doing an incredible move if they had a yo-yo tied around one of their fingers. The champion of the most recent year of the competition won with one of these moves that he called Wonder Woman's Backyard BBQ. It's named this because his wrists appear to go completely rigid (as if wearing Wonder Woman's metal bracelets) for the final ten seconds of movement. In reality, he is moving his hands and wrists too fast for the unaided eye to perceive. The speed of his hands causes the air around him to heat up to temperatures comparable to the interior of a vintage charcoal grill. Also, in the final moment of the move, the ball is spinning on the end of a string that has been woven into a perfect image of Lynda Carter wrestling Gal Gadot for a freshly grilled hamburger.

SUPERTASTERS

When someone eats something and has a big reaction, that's gay.

Supertasters have such a sensitive palate that it actually can't take constructive criticism. They are tied with musical theater kids for the most annoying type of person you'll ever be around.

Supertasters' palates are empaths, so they don't have to take responsibility for the way they respond to things, because they're just reflecting what's around them.

Supertasting originally came from soup culture, which is gay. In most communities, there used to be one person in town who could tell you what your soup was missing, and that person was a Supertaster.

Nowadays, Supertasters take their profession very seriously, even using a tongue sock when not eating, like hand models do with gloves.

Their discerning palate is also used in settings outside the culinary world:

+ Used in the NFL to make sure no one has been filling the Gatorade cooler with Vitamin Water to turn players gay.
+ Used by Area 51 to see what aliens taste like.
+ Used by Tyra Banks on the set of ANTM so she could "just know what her models taste like."

Supertaster goes beyond the tongue. You can have supertaste in a specific subject, i.e., Bonnie McKee is a supertaster of pop music.

There are also people called Supertastemakers, one of which was hired to help JVN fabricate the personality of an icon.

And then, of course, there's SuperWalmart, a place created in 1988 for customers to get lost and die in.

THE GAY HEART

The typical gay heart has five chambers, one more than a straight heart. This fifth chamber contains a very small choir called a **chamber choir**. The choir is told that, if they sing a song compellingly enough, one day they will be released and get to be revealed from behind a curtain to perform the final chorus of a popular song with a bestselling artist at the Grammy Awards. When you see a gay person and can just tell they have a song in their heart, this is why.

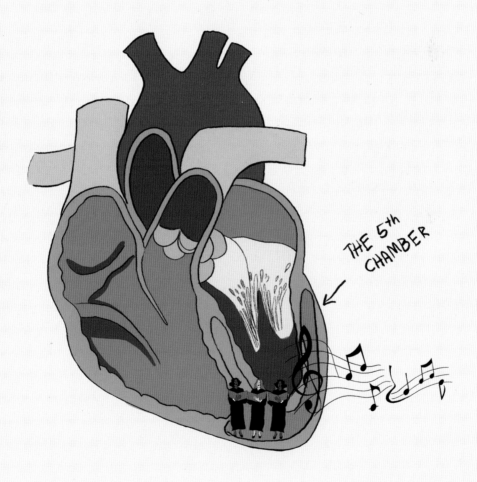

THE 5th CHAMBER

THE MANY BIOLOGICAL SHORTCOMINGS OF HETEROSEXUAL BODIES

In comparison to queer ones, heterosexual bodies have several obvious and inherent flaws in their composition.

+ In straight people's pores, there are little, microscopic creatures who are obsessed with getting them to put on an episode of the show *Friends*.
+ Straight men's bodies are excruciatingly sensitive to products, especially hygiene products, that are not specifically marketed toward men. If they use products that are marketed for women or without gender in mind, they will become very, very sick.
+ Straight people have less developed eyesight and cannot see the color **Blumbkel**. For gay people, this is likely hard to believe, but it's true. The color Blumbkel is imperceptible to straights. Many do not even think Blumbkel is a thing at all.
+ The aforementioned wig-fly incompetence.
+ Straight brains have 55 percent less room for secrets. The section of the brain responsible for secret storage, the Orimble Croxata, in straight brains is small and weak and can only be strengthened through a complicated series of risky surgical procedures.
    + Straight people have a small switch behind their left ear that will play The Counting Crows at a volume only they can hear. If the switch is flipped, the music will not stop until they have married their high school sweetheart, with whom they are completely incompatible.
    + Straight men medically need to drink all but the last tenth of a Gatorade and leave the bottle somewhere without finishing it or throwing it away.

Moisturizer For
MEN

Kills 10% of the microscopic creatures that love Friends!

CARDBOARD BOX AS NIGHTSTAND

CLAUDIUS: THE FIRST GAY SURGEON

Claudius Parker became a surgeon by accident in an age when there were no gay surgeons, 2012. He was an extra on the set of Shonda Rhimes's hit series *Grey's Anatomy* and was playing, of all things, a surgical *patient*, when one of the boom operators suddenly collapsed. The boom operator began calling out that he needed surgery as soon as possible. He wasn't sure what for, but he knew it was urgent and kept crying out that it was "sort of an intuitive thing." The entire crew began furiously searching through the crowd of actors dressed as doctors (this episode was set during a huge doctor convention) trying to find even one real doctor, or a person involved with the show who knew of or had maybe met a real doctor before. No one was able to help, until Claudius stood from his hospital bed. Just as the boom operator had claimed his intuition was telling him he needed surgery, Claudius's intuition began telling him that the operation was gay in nature and needed to be performed by a gay person, trained in medicine or not.

"I'm gay!" Claudius announced.

The crew thought this was an irrelevant and frankly inappropriate announcement at a time like this, but Claudius was already making his way to the writhing boom operator. Crew members tried to stop him, until the boom operator went eerily still and said, "No. Let him come."

The crew allowed Claudius through, despite their justifiable reservations, because the boom operator had spoken with such conviction that they couldn't bring themselves to refuse him. On a Shonda Rhimes set, speaking with conviction will always take precedence over reason and common sense. Claudius began calling for tools he knew from having watched the show in preparation for his role as an extra. Crew members and cast members alike began passing him scalpels, gauze, clamps, anything he could think of. After an hour of intuitive surgery, Claudius shook the blood from his bare, un-gloved hands and looked up at the crowd of people gathered around him.

"He's going to make it," Claudius reassured the crowd and the cameras.

Because the entire event had been caught on film, The Board of Medicine soon found out about Claudius's surgery and bestowed upon him the title of Premiere Intuitive Gay Surgeon. He was the first gay person to ever perform surgery and, after that, gay enrollment in medical schools around the world went up three million percent. At the time of publishing, many of those students are just finishing school, and it won't be long before the world sees its second gay surgeon and hopefully hundreds more.

SHOWMANSHIP IN NATURE

To illustrate the effects of showmanship in Nature, we've pulled an old stand-up set from Hannah Gadsby before she started working on *Nanette*:

Spiders show off with their webs, birds show off with their mating rituals, beavers show off with their dams, the flowers show off with their sights and smells. The Grand Canyon is gratuitous. Mount Everest? Really took it to a ten with that one. Peacocks are obnoxious with their in-your-face attitude. You can have a certain lifestyle, but you don't need to shove it in other people's faces. Diamonds need too much attention, like truly, get over yourself. You think you're special because you were formed under pressure? That's very capitalistic of you. Very Jeff Bezos.

Hey, crystal formations, are you trying to be diamonds or something? You're showing off! Does Nature have no shame?

An ant can lift like ten thousand more times than it weighs. Awesome, get them into a circus? I literally don't know what you want from me.

I get that water can be frozen, liquid, and a gas. It's like, pick a lane! You need to choose one thing, or people aren't going to know you for anything, babe. It's extra, I'm sorry. But we can all agree. I see through all of it. What do you need, Nature? Did the other planets make fun of you while you were developing? Sorry. I'm just saying it. No one else will talk about it. I just say what everyone else is thinking.

And lightning!

Lightning is so loud. And bright! Like, there are people trying to sleep . . . At some points it's like, well now this is just for you. It's not even for me anymore. The showmanship is unmatched. It's unmatched! I'll give Nature that. I'll concede that to them. But watch Nature take that and run with it. Give an inch and Nature will take a mile. Am I right?

BIOLOGY

HORSES ARE SO SASSY

Horses are in *The Lord of the Rings*. They are around little rich girls all the time. So, yeah, they've developed a bit of an attitude.

We dare not do anything but accept the sassy nature of the horse. They can sense your greatest weakness and aren't afraid to turn it against you at a party in front of your friends. Their hair is so beautiful that it unconsciously draws you in to touch it. Do you want to mess with that kind of power? A beast with an incredibly saucy attitude developed over thousands of years of being the sole focus of spiritual paintings. They can sense the attention. They're not fucking idiots. They're horses.

Miranda Priestly from *The Devil Wears Prada* trembles when speaking to a horse.

"AN APPLE A DAY KEEPS THE DOCTOR AWAY."
—HORSES

In fact, only rich people can afford to have horses, because a horse actually won't hang out with you if you don't have money. They're openly classist, but who is going to stop them? A peasant like you?

When adolescent girls are obsessed with you, you're entitled to behave however you please. Look at Justin Bieber. He pissed in a bucket because that's what a horse does when it wants attention. Coincidentally, horses also find God in their late twenties.

Horses are also famously well-endowed. They have massive penises, can run so fast, and have beautiful hair. It's incredibly understandable how all of this would go to your head. Did you want them to be shy about it? If you don't support how sassy horses are, there's something going on inside of yourself that you need to examine. Horses paved the way for the self-love movement. No one celebrates themselves more than horses do. They're also incredibly healthy. They love apples.

Megan Thee **Stallion**, a beloved cultural icon. Is it a surprise that she's one of the most influential artists of our lifetime? Embracing herself fully. Her sexuality, her body. Megan has the metaphorical horse cock with the confidence of a true stallion.

Horses have been key features for all our important pop culture: Cowboys. Elves. Music. Film/TV. Spirituality. Paintings. They can act however they please, and they're not going anywhere. What are you going to do? Tell off a horse? Well, there's a reality competition show where you can try it called *Piss Off a Horse*. Be our guest.

SURE, BEARS ARE "HIBERNATING"...

Do you believe that bears are hibernating during the winter months?

Do you believe in Santa Claus?

Bears are not hibernating. Bears are having gay sex for three months. It's a lot of gay sex. Like, so much gay sex.

The amount of gay sex bears are having would put Dan Savage to shame. Imagine how many grains of sand there are on Earth. That's the amount of gay sex bears are having instead of hibernating. It's the only way we can describe it. Here's an artist's rendition of what it looks like in the bear cave for three straight months:

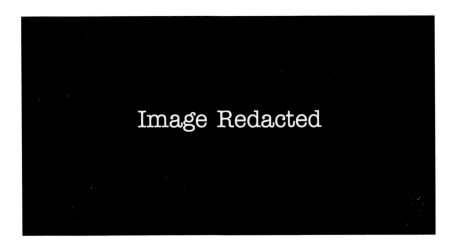

Bears have gay sex for three straight months, *that's* why they need to put on so much weight beforehand. They're going to need it.

They don't really take breaks for water or anything, they just go for a long time. Non-stop gay sex from bears.

Bears love honey because they use it as lube. Sorry if that creates an uncomfortable feeling in your body or a disturbing image. It's just science.

It's—we can't even begin to help you fathom the enormous amount of energy that is spent on the even larger amount of gay sex taking place between bears during the winter months.

We hope this has been eye-opening. It's time for the world to know the truth.

THE CREEPING NATURE OF IVY

It's green, it's creepy. It's not the over-sexualized green M&M. It's ivy. A plant that can grow on the side of a house and make it mysterious yet charming, an energy that a lot of men with acoustic guitars *think* they're giving off. The energy that compels ivy to attach itself to a Victorian home is actually the same energy that compels a gay couple to renovate a brownstone. Ivy is Nature's mural. Not to mention, ivy is a huge component of cottagecore, one of the gayest aesthetics the world has ever seen.

But where does ivy come from?

Back in the early 1800s, there was a very creepy old man known in his town as Mister Shivers. Mister Shivers was the town florist, a strange old man who had shared some intense relationships with his "roommates" during the war. This is actually where the euphemism for a gay cohabitating relationship came from. He was alone in his old age and had survived many a gardening accident, one of them piercing his right eye (the gay eye you get pierced), leaving him with a glass eye, which is equivalent to today's dangly statement earring. Unfortunately, he was also extremely creepy. His garden was the most beautiful the town had ever seen, but no one ever visited because of his creeping nature, and there was a rumor going around that if you smelled his roses, they would turn you "fancy."

> "I'M A CREEP,
> I'M A WEIRDO."
>
> —IVY

Mister Shivers had always wanted to share his garden with the world but never had the opportunity to do so during his life. He died alone in his beautiful garden after receiving a letter from an old lover, which said he had started a monthly newsletter called *Better Homes* that was doing quite well, and he wondered if Lewis (Mister Shivers) would like to be a part of it with a section called *and Gardens*. Mister Shivers died from being too touched by a letter he received, one of the gayest ways you can die.

With no one checking on him, his garden engulfed his gay old body and lovingly incorporated him into the soil. His DNA mixed with one of the weeds in the garden, and a new vine-like plant began to grow and creep into the neighbors' yards. It was ivy. The townspeople admired the ivy for its enigmatic beauty and melancholic presence. Soon the ivy became a hot commodity for those with little to no original taste who wanted to spruce up their home, like shiplap or a sliding barn door for a bathroom. Thankfully, ivy has withstood the test of time and ever-changing trends, remaining one of the most beautiful things you can add to a home besides a gay child.

Mister Shivers taught us a valuable lesson: If you're gay and weird, keep going. You could be the next big thing.

WHY THE WOODS
ARE SCARY

The woods are scary because they're gay, even though straight men feel drawn there. The woods were meant to be a safe space for young gay boys to sneak off and kiss in, but it's also where thousands of straight men flock to wander for a year after dropping out of their undergraduate programs. This is known as the Patagonia Paradox.

The woods have made themselves scary because too many corporations have created hetero-male–targeted body washes with scents inspired by them. Trees do not want to be appropriated by straight male culture, so they are fighting back. They are scaring you. Fir, pine? These are meant to be faggy scents, and they've been *stolen* from the musk of the trees. The woods want straights to know they're not safe there. However, if you are a woman in a white dress, riding a white horse, you are ok, and the woods will no longer be scary.

If you haven't read the section on what bears are doing instead of hibernating, it will give you a better picture of just how gay the woods really are. Not to be like this, but let's make the woods gay again.

EVOLUTION IS A COMPETITION AND SO IS BEING GAY

Evolution is the theory of life developing over time with an unexplained, intrinsic guide. An intrinsic guide that can be a bit fussy. Are we, as humans, intrinsically fussy? Call it Evolution, call it The Kinsey Scale: our DNA can't go a generation without trying to adjust. Evolution is design. Design is gay. Evolution is gay. Design is a competition, thanks to HGTV. Evolution is designing life. Evolution is essentially putting a room together. DNA mutations are tchotchkes. Therefore, Evolution is not only gay, it's also a competition.

However, the most important takeaway is that Evolution is inherently gay because it gave male-bodied humans a prostate.

WATERFALLS: WHEN WATER WANTS ATTENTION

What can't water do? It creates life, it nourishes, it's the reason we're all here. People flock from thousands of miles away to go lay by it all day. It's the reason places like Nobu exist. But even the greats of this world sometimes need attention, like when Harry Styles pretends to be queer. That's where waterfalls come into play.

In movies, we've seen characters in desperate need of love and affection threaten to throw themselves from a very high place. It's the most dramatic thing anyone or thing can do, and it's how we got our first waterfall. Not many things could hurl themselves down hundreds of feet and remain intact and utterly perfect. In fact, a waterfall cleans the water. Water took a dramatic cry for attention and turned it into self-care.

Nothing will grab your attention like a waterfall. You could be hiking with your partner, having the worst fight of your relationship, but when you reach the waterfall, y'all both shut up and gaze in awe. That's exactly what the water wants.

Why does water need attention? All life comes from attention. The more attention, the more life. Now, you'll notice most waterfalls are hard to reach and can take hours to hike to, so why would waterfalls be there if they need so much attention? Well, as we all know, it's not quantity, it's quality that counts. If someone walks two hours up the side of the mountain just to come see you and take photos with you . . . you're going to feel quite special.

Would anyone in history have ever done anything if it didn't get them attention? Sure, but those people are incredibly dull to be around. They don't start any drama and they're considerate. Water is not considerate—have you ever seen a hurricane? That happens when not enough people are visiting the waterfalls. Hurricanes are water acting out.

Perhaps that's where humans get their need for attention. We are 90 percent water after all.

THE RINGS OF A TREE

The rings of a tree measure how attracted that tree is to the superhero, elemental warrior, and queer icon Captain Planet. Older trees tend to have more rings, both because they begin having a more nuanced understanding of their desires as they age, and because, like a fine wine, Captain Planet gets more juicy, rich, and flavorful every year. You know how some wines need time to open up? Think about how, after a bit of time, Captain Planet—you know, forget it.

Every tree, regardless of age, is attracted to Captain Planet, despite him being a humanoid elemental warrior and not another tree. It would be hard not to be. He is gorgeous. That body! That hair! His smile! But the rings of a tree coincide specifically with how attractive they would find Captain Planet if he were also a tree. Hypothesizing over what a supernatural being's tree form would be like may strike you as deeply subjective, but in Captain Planet's case, it is widely agreed that, as a tree, he would be way sexy and way hot. One of the sexiest and hottest trees. Just a total smoke show of a tree. Are you understanding? Remember how everyone felt about Carmen Electra in the 2000s? Like that is how the trees feel about Captain Planet, if he were also a tree and not a combination of the powers of five elemental forces harnessed by young gay conservationists.

The oldest trees on record are said to have upwards of ten thousand rings. These trees should not be allowed anywhere near Captain Planet. At this point, oaks that fall into the nine- to ten-thousand ring range present a danger to the hero. Their lust for the Cartoon Warrior has morphed into an untamable obsession. Stephen King said in a 1990 interview that his novel *Misery* was based on what he thought a ten-thousand-ring tree might do to Captain Planet if it were alone with him. The oldest trees in one of Planet's favorite cities, San Juan, would slaughter each other so that they could have paper ready for an autograph in case the hero happened to walk by. Planet's international tour managers have gone to great lengths to assure that he never ventures to the Pacific Northwest, for fear that he would not survive an encounter with a redwood. Planet's fear of the trees since this information has come to light has also caused him a change of heart on many conservation issues. Recently, he has invested hundreds of thousands of dollars to fight those fighting deforestation.

"At a certain point, the climate and maintenance of important ecosystems began to feel less important to me than making sure a bristlecone pine doesn't break my ankles," Planet said while promoting his 2016 memoir, *Making Peace with Exxon*, which largely focuses on the growth of his intimate and personal relationships with a large number of the industry titans destroying the environment, and his journey toward mindfulness as he conditioned himself to sleep comfortably with a commercial-grade wood chipper running next to his bed.

Trees seem generally unfazed by Planet's public distaste for them. In a 2017 tweet, a pine tree sapling described the blue cartoon man as "un-cancelable," going on to say, "I want him to snap me in half like the worthless twig I am."

ANCIENT TREE COULDN'T HANDLE CAPTAIN PLANET'S BEAUTY

MITOSIS AND THE NEED TO ADOPT TWINS

Mitosis is the process by which a cell divides into two identical daughter cells. It is a very new process. Cells first began going through mitosis in 2016, after that federal district court struck down the ban on same-sex couples adopting children in Mississippi. This historic precedent for the United States resulted in a boom in adoptions of children by same-sex couples, inevitably leading to the massive number of gay couples with twins. Gay couples just love adopting twins. There is something in the genetic engineering of gay brains that releases copious amounts of serotonin at the mere idea of adopting *two* children who've shared a uterus. This desire stems from the core queer impulse to have a backup of something "just in case."

When cells found out that this long-overdue decision was made supporting the right of gay couples nationwide to adopt children (and inevitably many, many sets of twins), cells collectively felt it was only right that they show their allyship in a big way. Cell leaders decided that they would show their support by splitting in a new way, meant to reflect how 100 percent behind the idea of gay adoption they were, but more specifically how much they felt it was "awesome" for so many gay couples in America to finally live out their dream of raising "two very well-behaved twins." After weeks of preparation, cells unveiled mitosis via a series of Instagram stories in collaboration with Demi Lovato, set to their hit song, "Cool for the Summer." They described it as a "cool new move in the cell reproduction space that was so gay and totally 2016."

Mitosis ended up being a very efficient cell reproduction method despite initially being just for show, and today many cells divide through mitosis for simply utilitarian purposes. Some cells born through mitosis today wouldn't even know that mitosis had its roots in celebration of a 2016 legal milestone for gay Americans and in the career of pop icon Demi Lovato.

HEY BABE! I GRABBED TWO JUST IN CASE!

BACTERIA: A TESTAMENT TO QUEER RESILIENCE

Bacteria are gay, and because of that, they are some of the most resilient organisms, if not *the* most resilient organisms, in our universe. Gayness physically, spiritually, and culturally fortifies an organism for survival under the most extreme and unforgiving conditions. This is why bacteria are found nearly everywhere on earth, even in its cruelest and most inhospitable places. This is, similarly, why some gay Americans somehow still find it possible to thrive and lead full, rich, creative lives in rural parts of the American Midwest.

Humans have ten times as many bacterial cells as they do human cells. It naturally follows that everyone is ten times gayer than they are human. It's important to keep that in mind as we consider, culturally, what unites us. Specifically, as we consider one of our most pervasive cultural artifacts: those shirts that list sexualities or races and have all of them crossed out and then the word "Human" written underneath. It would be more apt to have a shirt with "human" listed among a number of other closely-held identities: Daughter, American, Grammy Nominee; with all of those crossed out and "Gay" scrawled underneath.

QUIZ

Is This Rock Gay?

At this point in the text, the reader should have a clear enough understanding of the many nuanced indicators of gayness to identify it in the world around them. This Quiz will help test your skills and reveal where there may be room for more growth and research. Your score on a quiz like this is a direct reflection of your self-worth, and we hope that your performance here informs your sense of personal value, or lack thereof, for at least the rest of the day. Happy quizzing.

ANSWERS

1. No, this rock is not gay. This rock is wearing black dress socks with gym sneakers.
2. Yes, this rock is gay. This rock is wearing black dress socks with gym sneakers but in an ironic trendy way.
3. Yes, this rock is gay; it is actually a crystal that allows the viewer to peer into the future.
4. No, this rock is not gay. It is a crystal that allows the viewer to peer into another dimension but in a Rick and Morty type of way that seems to pander to teen incels who think they are smarter than everyone because they listened to one podcast about string theory two years ago.
5. Yep. They're gay!
6. No, this rock is not gay. It is pretending to be gay for attention on TikTok and it is working.
7. No, this rock is not gay. It is really into the show *Rent*, but in a weirdly straight way, because the rock's high school did a production and cast the rock as Roger, and this rock used his performance of "One Song Glory," to work out a lot of anger he was having about women in general.
8. Yes, this rock is a gay therapist. The rock can provide really fantastic insight into a world a gay person may have to waste a lot of time explaining to a straight therapist. This rock is a hero.
9. No, this rock is not gay, it is asexual, and that's ok too.

GAY BUGS

Every part of the anatomical composition of an insect reinforces the vital truth that bugs are some of PAUL's gayest creations.

EXOSKELETON

Bugs have a durable, exterior skeleton that not only supports but also protects the soft tissue within. For bugs, this firm exterior betrays that, inside, they are sensitive, impressionable, fleshy, queer angels. The exoskeleton is effectively a *Maxim* magazine being held in front of a book of poetry. It is a suit of armor shielding the fact that the body beneath is decorated with three to five script tattoos of Kate Bush lyrics. The exoskeleton is the pickup truck that has a 24-pack of strawberry-kiwi ChapStick hidden in the glove compartment. Sometimes, when it feels safe, a bug will bang against its hard exoskeleton trying to do the drum solo from the beginning of "Lose My Breath" by Destiny's Child.

THREE-PART BODY

Swedish pop singer and gay icon Robyn released her album *Body Talk* in three parts to represent the three segments of the body of a bug. Bugs demographically make up 95 percent of her fan base and Robyn has gone on record multiple times saying how grateful she is for her gay fans, particularly the hundreds of thousands of bugs who stream her music constantly.

THREE PAIRS OF JOINTED LEGS

Insects have six legs that function in three pairs. This is so they can individually perform elaborate tap routines that typically would need to be performed by three separate humans. The show *42nd Street* can be performed believably in its entirety by only four insects. A Broadway revival of the musical starring some of the leading cast members of *A Bug's Life* has been in development for the past six years.

COMPOUND EYES

Insects have compound eyes made up of many simple eyes operating as a collective unit. This sort of collaborative functionality requires that the eyes be gay. It would not be possible for the compound eye to be composed of many *straight* simple eyes, because the straight eyes would be too busy loudly talking over each other trying to explain the plot of *Fight Club* instead of doing any of the actual perceiving they were intended to do.

ONE PAIR OF ANTENNAE

Bug antennae are Nature's most powerful gaydars. They are instinctually drawn to gay energy. When a bug is on you, it's because you've been acting gay.

WIND AND WEATHER PATTERNS SPREADING GAY MESSAGES

Sometimes, as a gay person, it will feel as if the wind is speaking to you. It is. The wind is in fact carrying a message from one of your queer ancestors, letting you know who was sort of acting like a bitch in the summer of 1284. This will most likely feel unimportant, since it is now so many years in the future, and whomever was behaving badly is likely dead. You're right, but they are your queer ancestors, so it's important to humor them and performatively say something like, "Yeah, it seems like he was way out of line there. You're totally justified in feeling that way" into the wind in the hopes it will be at peace.

WENDY WILLIAMS   PLOT OF *HEREDITARY*

Checks in on how we're doin'

Very public mistakes and apologies
to LGBTQ+ community

I'm a little scared but
I'm having a good time

We are memorizing
the iconic speeches

Yelling

Abruptly revealing
someone has died

Death to all of them!

Not interested in how we're doin'

LGBTQ+ people just don't exist
in this world I guess?

GRAPH OF HOW GAY CHARTS ARE

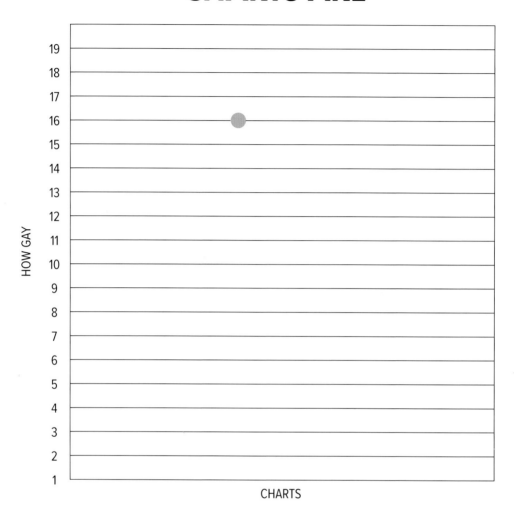

CHART OF HOW GAY GRAPHS ARE

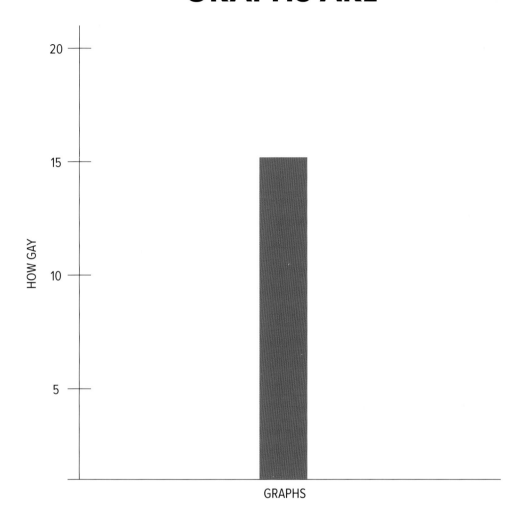

Charts are slightly gayer because of the hard "ch" sound at the beginning of the word "charts." Just like "cherish," which is one of the gayest sounding words.

GLOBAL GAY VIBE OVER TIME

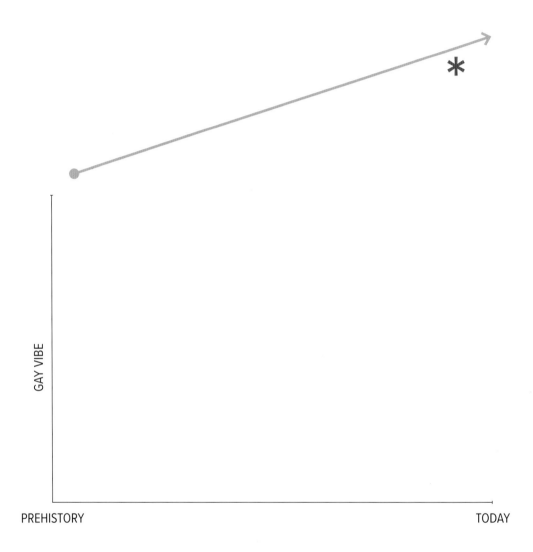

GAY VIBE

PREHISTORY

TODAY

✳ The world has always been off-the-charts gay

WHO IS SINGING RIGHT NOW

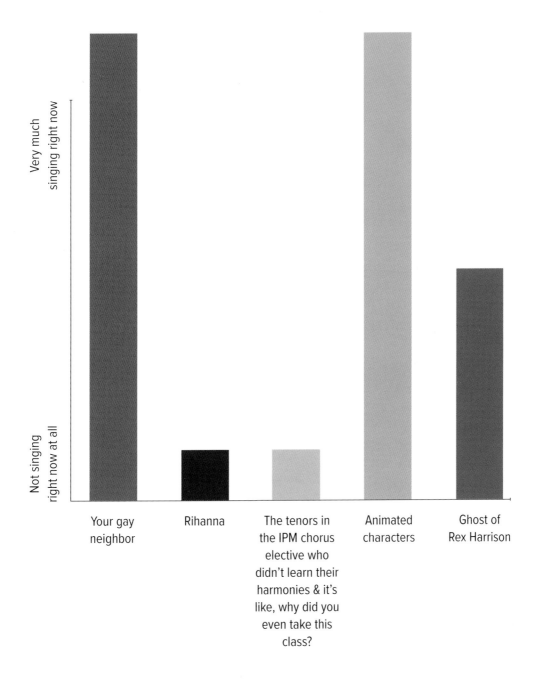

Very much singing right now

Not singing right now at all

Your gay neighbor

Rihanna

The tenors in the IPM chorus elective who didn't learn their harmonies & it's like, why did you even take this class?

Animated characters

Ghost of Rex Harrison

HOW TO COME OUT

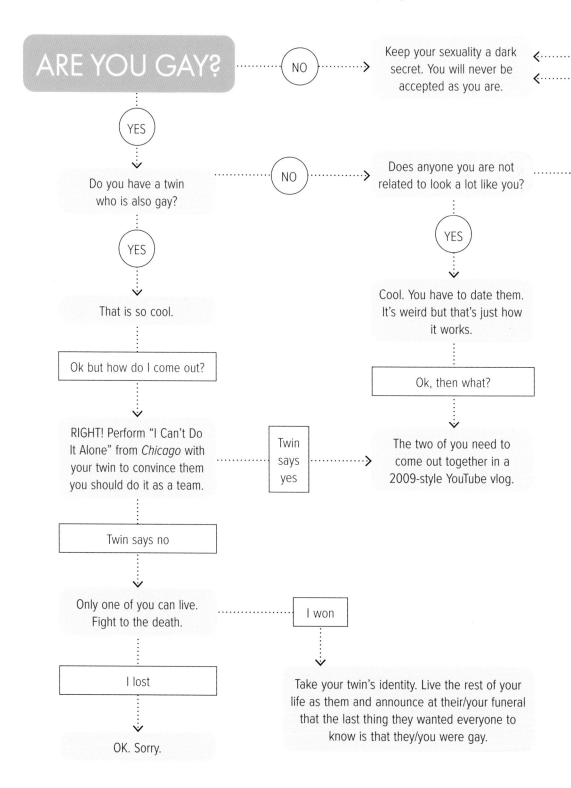

ARE YOU GAY? ·········· NO ·········> Keep your sexuality a dark secret. You will never be accepted as you are. <········· <·········

YES

Do you have a twin who is also gay? ·········· NO ·········> Does anyone you are not related to look a lot like you? ·········

YES

That is so cool.

Ok but how do I come out?

RIGHT! Perform "I Can't Do It Alone" from *Chicago* with your twin to convince them you should do it as a team. ·········· Twin says yes ·········>

YES

Cool. You have to date them. It's weird but that's just how it works.

Ok, then what?

The two of you need to come out together in a 2009-style YouTube vlog.

Twin says no

Only one of you can live. Fight to the death. ·········· I won

I lost

OK. Sorry.

Take your twin's identity. Live the rest of your life as them and announce at their/your funeral that the last thing they wanted everyone to know is that they/you were gay.

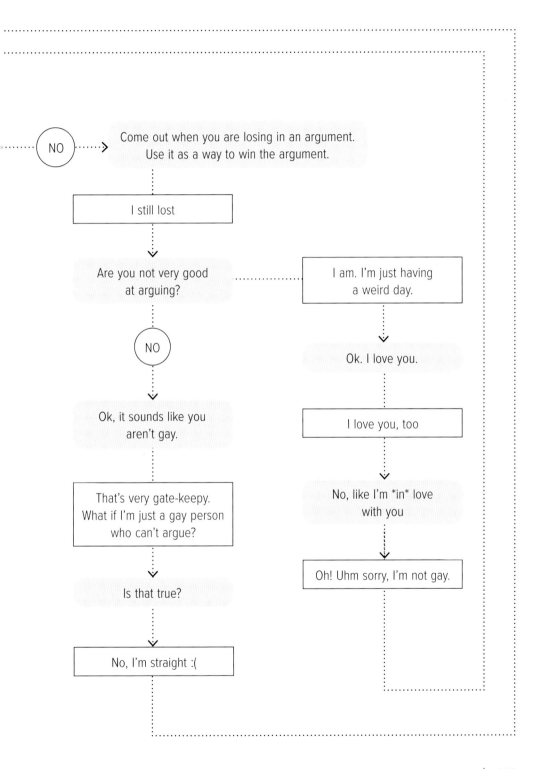

MERYL STREEP

MERYL STREEP

Meryl Streep

ACKNOWLEDGMENTS

We want to thank all of the incredible people who made this book possible. This could not have happened without the many powerful minds in our corner, some straight and some regular. Thank you to Adriana Stimola, who saw the potential in us as writers before we even knew how to read or write (we learned for this book!). Thank you to Allison Adler and Betty Wong for your keen eyes and insightful guidance. Thank you for helping mold what had only been an oral history into this concrete tome of eternal truths. Thank you to Lex Bohémier. A HUGE thank you to Bradley Clayton. Just when we thought this book couldn't be gayer, we found you and your perfect, gay brain. Thank you for giving shape and color to the insane world we've described in these pages. You are a dream. Finally, thank you to every gay person for not writing this book before us. Honestly, that would've been really fucked up.

ABOUT THE AUTHORS

Nicholas Scheppard and **Jenson Titus** are thousands of years old and no one really knows where they came from. Most recently, their project Very Gay Paint has gained notoriety for being a perfect mix of comedy and interior design.